About the Author

Dr Vernon Coleman worked as a GP in the Midlands for ten years. He is now a professional author and broadcaster. He was the UK's first TV agony uncle, has made three TV series based on his best-selling book *Bodypower* and has made a special series of programmes on tranquillisers to accompany *Life Without Tranquillisers*. His weekly medical columns appear in newspapers all over the world. He is the author of over thirty books which have been translated into eleven languages. Four have been in the 'bestseller' lists. He is a Fellow of the Royal Society of Medicine.

By the same author:

On Medicine

The Medicine Men
Paper Doctors
Everything You Want to Know About Ageing
Stress Control
The Home Pharmacy
Aspirin or Ambulance
Face Values
Stress and Your Stomach
Guilt
The Good Medicine Guide
A Guide to Child Health
Bodypower
An A-Z of Women's Problems
Bodysense
Taking Care of Your Skin
Life Without Tranquillisers
High Blood Pressure
Diabetes
Arthritis
Eczema and Dermatitis
The Story of Medicine

On Cricket

Thomas Winsden's Cricketing Almanack
Diary of a Cricket Lover

As Edward Vernon

Practice Makes Perfect
Practise What You Preach
⁺ Getting Into Practice
Aphrodisiacs – An Owner's Manual
The Complete Guide to Life

As Marc Charbonnier

Tunnel

MINDPOWER

How to use your mind to heal your body

Dr Vernon Coleman

CENTURY
LONDON MELBOURNE AUCKLAND JOHANNESBURG

First published as a paperback 1987
First published in 1986 by Century Hutchinson Ltd
Brookmount House, 62–65 Chandos Place, Covent Garden,
London WC2N 4NW

Century Hutchinson Australia Pty Ltd
16–22 Church Street, Hawthorn, Melbourne, Victoria 3122

Century Hutchinson New Zealand Ltd
32–34 View Road, PO Box 40-086, Glenfield, Auckland 10

Century Hutchinson South Africa Pty Ltd
PO Box 337, Bergvlei 2012, South Africa

British Library Cataloguing in Publication Data
Coleman, Vernon
Mindpower: how to use your mind to
heal your body.
1. Psychotherapy
I. Title
616.89'14   RC480

ISBN 0-7126-1563-6

Set in 11/12 Sabon by Deltatype, Ellesmere Port

Printed in Great Britain by
St Edmundsbury Press Ltd, Bury St Edmunds, Suffolk
Bound by Butler & Tanner Ltd, Frome and London

Contents

CHAPTER 1

The birth of an idea – the origins of mindpower

I've been interested in the power of the mind over the body for ten or fifteen years now. Nearly a decade ago one of the first books I ever wrote was on the subject of stress and the way that the human body can be damaged by pressure and anxiety. After exploring the reasons why stress is so prevalent in our society, I detailed the hundred and one different diseases that can be caused or made worse by one sort of pressure or another.

At that time I saw the effect of the mind on the body as being largely negative. I realized that contentment and happiness could reduce the risk of disease developing, but I didn't really comprehend the way in which the mind can have a healing as well as a damaging effect. I thought that happiness and other positive emotions were therapeutic only in so far as they kept stress at bay.

And then a couple of years after I'd written my book on stress I had a revelation. I was getting towards the end of a book promotion tour at the time and I was absolutely shattered. In the space of about two weeks I'd visited dozens of radio and television studios and talked to a variety of newspaper and magazine reporters. I'd covered hundreds of miles and stayed in all sorts of strange hotel rooms. I'd travelled by aeroplane, by train, by car and by foot. I'd answered the same questions a thousand times.

The book I was promoting at the time had absolutely nothing to do with stress – it was about how the beauty industry takes money from customers by selling them dreams and images rather than good, honest products – but during the

1

tour I'd experienced about as much stress as I could take. I was physically and mentally exhausted.

With about five days of the tour to go I woke up with a streaming cold. My throat was sore and my head ached. My legs, arms and back felt as though they'd been pummelled by a heavyweight boxing champion. I had the 'flu and I should have stayed where I was for a few days to recover.

But I still had several important interviews to do and I knew that the book was selling well. Everywhere I'd been there had been a tremendous amount of interest in the subject and every time I'd done a phone-in radio programme the lines had been blocked with callers. I knew that if I could just get through the next five days, I could then rest for as long as I liked. And I also knew that if I ended the tour prematurely, I would probably lose a good deal of the interest I'd stimulated. If only I could drag myself out of bed and carry on with the rest of the tour I would probably manage to arouse a lot more enthusiasm for the subject and, at the same time, sell a lot more books.

Feeling rather foolish, I lay there in bed and made a deal with my body and with the bug that had undoubtedly infected it. I told both of them that I needed five days of good health and that I couldn't spare the time to be ill until that five days had elapsed. I explained that I would be perfectly willing to put up with the 'flu after the five-day period was over. Then I got up, had a shower and got dressed.

By the time I was ready to get out on the road again I was feeling much better. My throat was no longer sore and my voice wasn't cracked and hoarse. My muscles felt fine and my headache had gone. My nose was unblocked and I was raring to go.

I got through the next five days without any trouble at all. I hit the radio and television stations precisely on time and I completed the schedule of arranged interviews. Everything went well and the book sold out and had to be reprinted.

And then, with the tour over, I went back home to rest for a while before starting work on my next manuscript. I already knew what I wanted to write, but I knew that I needed a short rest before I started work on it. I'd completely forgotten about the attack of 'flu and the deal I'd made with my body.

But my body hadn't forgotten. And nor had the 'flu bug disappeared. I'd hardly taken off my shoes before my throat started to feel sore again. My headache returned and my arms and legs began to feel heavy once more. My sniffles returned and within an hour or two I had all the symptoms that I'd had five days before.

At the time I didn't really take too much notice of what had happened. I was tired and I felt ill and I just wanted to rest. Since I had no more interviews to do, I just lay around for the next few days allowing my body to recover at its own pace.

It was only afterwards that I remembered the deal I'd made in the middle of the gruelling publicity tour. I remembered the way I'd felt when I'd woken up with five days of my tour to go. And I remembered the miraculous way in which the symptoms of the 'flu had disappeared.

It was then that, for the first time, I realized that the human mind has powers which are far more remarkable than I had ever before imagined. That single, isolated and in a way, I suppose, fairly insignificant incident, had opened my eyes to the fact that the mind has powers we have not yet begun to tap: powers that can control the way our bodies respond to disease and infection and powers that can be controlled in order to improve our health and well-being. Suddenly, all sorts of things started to fall into place and make sense.

For ten years after I qualified as a doctor, and before I started to earn my living as a professional author, I practised as a general practitioner. And during that time I found myself time and again dealing with patients who should have died but didn't. To a young medical student, brought up on the idea that science is all-powerful and that the human body responds to illness and pressure in fairly strictly defined ways, it was all very puzzling.

So, for example, there was Pam, a young woman who had cancer of the bowel and who should have died within a matter of weeks according to the hospital specialists who were involved in her care. But Pam didn't die. And she wouldn't even stay in hospital. She wasn't married, but she had three small children and insisted on going back home to look after them. The laboratory tests that the hospital doctors organized showed that she ought to have been dead, but she wasn't. She got thinner and thinner and began to look more and more like a skeleton, but still she didn't die.

Everyone involved in her care found it baffling. It was

3

indeed difficult to understand just what was keeping her alive. It certainly wasn't anything that anyone had prescribed for her. The drugs that had been offered had made her feel sick and she had steadfastly refused to continue with the treatment that had been recommended.

In the end, however, Pam got so weak that she agreed to go into the hospital for a short rest just as long as her children could be looked after by a family. That was, it suddenly seemed, the key to it all. She wouldn't even consider going into hospital if it meant that her three children had to be split up.

Finding a home for Pam's three children wasn't easy. The social workers I got in touch with wanted to split up the family and put the children into foster homes. There weren't any available homes that could cope with three new children all at the same time. But just as I was about to despair of ever finding an answer, a chance conversation with another patient led to a solution. A foster family was found where the three children could be cared for together. And so Pam went into hospital and her children went to stay with temporary foster parents.

While she was in hospital, the children went to see Pam every day. In response to her constant fears and questions, they told her that they were happy and comfortable. They talked about the things they'd done with their foster parents and of the places they'd visited. They were missing her, but they were settled and they were together. To my surprise, Pam didn't insist on leaving the hospital. She seemed happy to stay there for the time being.

And then one day she asked me to find out whether the children could stay with the foster parents indefinitely. The answer was an emphatic 'yes'. The foster parents had quickly fallen in love with their new family. They didn't want to be parted from them.

Pam died that day. It was as though she had held on to life all that time simply in order to make sure that her children were going to be all right. She had defied medical science through will-power, through a strong determination to stay alive until she was satisfied that her children were going to be well looked after and able to stay together as a family unit. And once her fears for them had been assuaged, she had let go of life and succumbed to the cancer that should have taken her life weeks or months before.

4

Pam hadn't been the only such patient, of course. There had been countless others. Each time I'd managed to convince myself that what had happened had been an exception, that the laboratory results must have been wrong, that there must have been some other unknown factors. Each time I had resisted the temptation to believe that there could have been some stronger, internal force involved in defying or doing a deal with death.

It wasn't just my own personal experiences as a general practitioner that had begun to convince me that the power of the mind over the body can be far greater than I had ever been taught possible. All my life I've read everything I could lay my hands on. I've devoured books and journals with a permanent appetite for the unusual. And all through the late 1960s and 1970s I'd come across countless authors claiming that the human mind can have a great influence on the things we do and the way we live.

To start with, much of the material I'd read had been anecdotal and fairly easy to dismiss. Together with most other doctors, I'd been sceptical of stories of Eastern yogis stopping their hearts beating or walking on beds of red-hot coals. I'd been intrigued but not convinced. Doctors are taught to be cynical and sceptical and I'd majored in both specialities. I wouldn't believe anything until I'd seen it proved beyond doubt.

But much of the material I'd come across wasn't quite so easy to dismiss. In 1972, for example, two American researchers, one the Assistant Professor of Medicine at Harvard Medical School, published results which showed that during meditation oxygen consumption and metabolic rates markedly decreased and that it was possible to measure a reduction in the level of anxiety recorded by people meditating. From France there was evidence from physiologists to prove that some people can slow or even stop their hearts while meditating. In 1970 *The Lancet* had published research showing that breathing rates per minute drop significantly during meditation. German research workers at the University of Cologne showed that people meditating reduced their levels of aggression, depression, irritability and nervousness.

There was a veritable deluge of similar material being published. All around the world researchers were finding that the human mind can have all sorts of positive effects on the body and that by learning to control the mind it is possible to control the way the body responds. Not that I'm pretending that all this material was new, of course. People had been arguing that the mind can affect the body for decades. It was just that the more I looked around, the clearer became the signs that this wasn't just hypothetical nonsense; it was valuable material that the medical profession was choosing to ignore.

When I began to look back at the way that medicine had been practised several thousand years ago I discovered that it had been very well established then that the power of the mind over the body can be quite dramatic. In India, for example, four or five thousand years ago flowers, perfumes and music therapy were used to make convalescence more enjoyable and successful. The Greek physician Hippocrates, frequently described as the father of modern medicine, understood that the individual's mind has a tremendous influence over what illnesses he develops and what happens to him when he develops those illnesses. Living over two thousand years ago, Hippocrates had understood the value of meditation and mental relaxation. He had recognized that the mind can have a tremendous, positive power over the body.

While I was finding new evidence to support the developing theory of 'mindpower' just about everywhere I looked, I was also finding myself face to face with just as many questions as answers. So, for example, when I was still a general practitioner, I remember an elderly lady coming into the surgery and asking me to give her something to stop her getting a winter cold. She said she didn't want any of the ordinary things such as 'flu vaccines or vitamin tablets, but she wanted one of the special remedies.

Puzzled, I asked her what she meant.

'I want what you doctors use,' she told me. 'You sit there all winter and get coughed on and sneezed at and yet you never get colds.'

I couldn't help her, of course. There is no special remedy that doctors use to protect themselves. And yet what she said had more than a little truth in it. Doctors, particularly in general practice, do spend an awful lot of time sitting directly in front of patients who are sneezing and spluttering and firing germs all over the place. And yet only rarely do general practitioners seem to catch colds. During my ten years of practice, for example, I only ever got a common or garden cold when I was away from the hurly-burly of daily practice. I could sit in the firing line for three months without getting a cold and then I would go away for a long weekend and come back with a running nose and streaming eyes.

Nor is this just true of the common cold. Doctors who work with patients suffering from other infectious diseases rarely seem to develop those deseases. Missionaries who work with patients suffering from all sorts of horrible bugs stay remarkably healthy when they should be falling sick. Why? That was just one of a hundred different questions I found myself unable to answer. And just one of a hundred questions that I desperately wanted to be able to answer.

By the early 1980s I felt that I was getting close to an explanation that would solve all those unanswered questions and enable me to understand just how patients like Pam had managed to stay alive when they should have died, just why I'd been able to throw off my 'flu bug while on my book promotion tour, and why patients with apparently identical bodies and apparently similar stresses should thrive and suffer in such very different ways.

I began to suspect that something had gone sadly wrong with orthodox medicine, that my training had been misleading and that all of us, doctors and patients, have become so obsessed with the mechanical wonders of modern science that we have lost our way.

CHAPTER 2

Traditional influences and medical practices

My first book, published in 1975, had been a highly critical attack on the drugs industry. I had exposed the many ways in which doctors are misled by drug companies and encouraged to prescribe products which are neither safe nor effective. At the time, the book had caused a furore within the medical profession. Doctors had attacked me violently for daring to suggest that they ever prescribed products which were unsafe.

My second book, published a year or so later, had taken me one step further. I had investigated the world of medical research and come to the then startling conclusion that medical researchers were contributing very little to the quality of health care, but were simply amassing new information and filling libraries with research papers which had little practical value. Medical researchers were, I concluded, inspired by personal and commercial motives and were accumulating information for all the wrong reasons.

But even though I had found much fault with the drug industry and the research 'industry', I still hadn't really found out why the medical profession was so out of touch. And it was clear that the profession wasn't just out of touch; it was completely failing to deal with the health problems of the twentieth century.

In the nineteenth century the medical profession had made enormous strides forward. At the beginning of that century life expectancy was low and millions of babies and young children never grew to adulthood. Diseases such as smallpox, typhoid, cholera and tuberculosis devastated whole communities. By the end of the century things had changed dramatically. Life expectancy had improved enormously and infants stood a much better chance of living to childhood and even adulthood. Improvements in public health facilities, in housing regulations, in food supplies and in agricultural policies had all helped to ensure that people had more to eat, better homes to live in, cleaner water to drink and greater protection against disease and infection.

By the start of the twentieth century the future looked bright. The drugs industry was just developing and surgical skills were being honed to new high standards. Anyone alive at the start of this century would have felt confident that the medical profession would bloom and that in future people would lead longer and healthier lives.

That hasn't happened. Within the last twenty years more money has been spent on medical care and research than had been spent in the whole of the rest of man's history on earth. Even allowing for inflation, that is a hell of a lot of money. Health care has become one of the world's largest and fastest growing industries. And yet we have virtually nothing to show for all the effort and money that has been expended. Very few important medical advances have been made in the last quarter of a century, and in those areas where advances have been made the work was begun decades ago.

Despite the fact that individual doctors remain committed to caring for the sick and the infirm, medicine has sunk into a slough and there has been almost no improvement in either the quality or the quantity of life enjoyed in the developed countries of the world. Indeed, the World Health Organization figures suggest that in some developed countries there has, in recent years, been a decrease in life expectancy and an increase in the mortality rate among young people.

Medicine has become full of confusions and paradoxes. Doctors keep a greater proportion of our over-65-year-olds and over-75-year-olds alive. But at the same time there has been an increase in the number of people dying in their thirties and forties. The expenditure on health care has rocketed in the developed countries. But the statistics suggest that people are now more likely to fall ill than they were a generation ago. The number of doctors goes up annually. But whenever doctors go on strike, the death rate goes down.

We have richer food supplies and more readily available

9

medicines today than ever before. But all the evidence suggests that in Britain people were never healthier than during the ravages of the Second World War. The government claims to recognize the value of preventive medicine. And yet in Britain half the adult population and a third of the child population take some form of medicament every day.

During the last quarter of a century we have developed remarkably sophisticated machinery for our hospitals. And yet cancers, immune disorders and allergy problems become commoner day by day. We now have specialist coronary care units for heart attack victims. And yet more people than ever are dying of heart disease. Young people are bigger and stronger than their ancestors. And yet the number of young children with diabetes is doubling every decade. More and more people are living in air-conditioned, centrally heated buildings. And yet infections still kill millions.

We have more surgeons and more operating theatres than ever before. And yet there are still enormous waiting lists for essential surgery. New procedures and drugs are tested far more effectively and extensively than ever before. And yet the incidence of doctor-induced disease continues to rise. There have never been so many rules to protect the rights of patients. And yet patients have never been so deprived of freedom. We have the technology to prevent unwanted pregnancies. And yet the demand for abortions never stops growing. Medicine has never been more sophisticated. And yet patients have never been so dissatisfied. Doctors have never tried harder, and never been less well loved.

There is no single, simple explanation for this disastrous state of affairs. In part, the problems are due to the fact that the medical profession has spent the last century creating a system of health care designed to suit its own needs rather than the needs of the patients. In part, the problems are due to the medical profession's failure to define or understand the real needs of the community.

But the overriding, essential fact is that doctors have taken too much control for themselves. Overcome with enthusiasm for the marvels of science, doctors have ignored the healing powers of the individual body and mind. Convinced by their own professional propaganda, they have built a profession which has too much respect for therapy and not enough

10

respect for healing. For the first time in history we have a medical profession with the power to interfere with nature. But for the first time in history we have a medical profession which has chosen to ignore the phenomenon of natural healing.

Doctors have become instilled with a sense of power and have taken too much responsibility. And out of a mixture of respect, admiration and fear, patients have let them take that responsibility. At the one time when we should be recognizing the remarkable curative and protective powers of the human mind, we have abdicated all responsibility and handed over our bodies to the technicians.

One of the most important reasons why doctors, as a group, have tended to ignore the natural healing powers of the human body and mind is because their attitude towards the body and towards illness was largely formulated by a seventeenth-century French philosopher called René Descartes, who believed that the human body is little more than a piece of machinery.

Following on from this Cartesian philosophy, the modern doctor believes that when something goes wrong, when symptoms develop or when the system is not functioning effectively, all you have to do is take the machine apart, examine all the bits and pieces and fiddle with those parts which are malfunctioning.

It is a simple, mechanistic approach which has served science well for several centuries. Modern surgical approaches and drug therapies have all been designed to help restore the smooth functioning of a machine which has been disrupted by infection or injury. The basic aim of most medical treatments is to suppress any signs and symptoms of illness or distress as quickly and as effectively as possible. A headache will be treated with a pain killer, indigestion will be treated with an antacid and high blood pressure will be treated with a drug designed to lower blood pressure.

Despite the fact that this philosophy has been responsible for many of the successes of modern medicine, there have for over a century been people who have not been convinced that Descartes got it completely right. There have, for example, been the many individuals who have pointed to the

11

remarkable ability of the human body to heal itself and have argued that, in view of what we know about the body's self-healing systems, a mechanistic approach is far too simplistic.

Following the early lead set by nineteenth-century French physiologist Claude Bernard and American physiologist W. B. Cannon, many researchers around the world have produced evidence to show that the body's internal mechanisms are designed to enable it to adapt to internal pressures and variations and to show that the most efficient healing systems in the world are to be found not in the doctor's pharmacy or the herbalist's garden, but inside the body itself.

Even the simplest available research evidence strongly suggests that the human body cannot be dismissed as a piece of simple machinery, but should instead be regarded as having an astonishing variety of internal self-healing systems. For example, consider what researchers have shown happens if you cut yourself. The first thing is that special proteins which circulate all the time in human blood automatically form a protective net designed to catch blood cells and form a clot designed to seal the wound and prevent further, unnecessary blood loss. (In fact, of course, the clotting system is more complex than that. There are a host of fail-safe devices which ensure that the system isn't accidentally triggered into action when there is no leak and that the clotting system doesn't begin to operate until enough blood has flown through an injury site to wash away any dirt and bacteria.)

Once the clotting system has ensured that the blood loss is kept to a minimum, another series of complex systems will guard against any potential risk of infection. As soon as a blood clot has formed and the loss of blood has been stopped, the damaged cells will release substances into the tissues, resulting in the expansion of the local blood vessels and the flow of extra quantities of blood into the injury site. This additional blood will make the area red, swollen and hot. The heat will help damage any infective organisms and the swelling will ensure that the injured part is not used too much. By immobilizing the area, the pain and stiffness will act as a natural splint.

White blood cells that are brought to the injury site will help by swallowing up any debris or bacteria which might still be there. Once they have done their job, these scavenging cells, bloated with rubbish, will allow themselves to be discharged from the body as pus. Once the injury begins to heal, the body shows an additional refinement. The scar tissue it builds will be much tougher than the original, damaged area of skin. Unsightly though it may be, the scar tissue ensures that the injured site is stronger than ever and better able to withstand any future injury.

Even when the body's blood clotting systems aren't quick enough or powerful enough to cope with damage without appreciable amounts of fluid escaping, all is not lost. Arteries supplying the injured area will constrict so as to limit further blood losses. Peripheral blood vessels supplying the skin will shut down so as to ensure that the supply of blood to the more essential organs can be preserved. The kidneys will cut the production of urine so that fluid levels in the body can be kept as high as possible. Fluids will be withdrawn from tissues to dilute and increase the amount of blood which remains. The red blood cell-producing site within the body will step up production in order to replace those cells which have been lost. Finally, as an added refinement, the loss of blood will trigger a thirst intended to make sure that the missing fluids are replaced as quickly as possible.

There are within every human body thousands of similar sophisticated protective systems. So, for example, we all have efficient temperature control devices so that wherever we happen to be – sitting on an ice floe or sweltering on a sand dune – our internal temperatures remain stable. If the outside temperature is too hot, we sweat and blood is diverted to our skin to increase the amount of heat that our bodies lose. If the outside temperature is cold, blood is diverted away from the skin in order to minimize the amount of internal heat being lost.

In the 1920s Dr Clara M. Davis of Chicago discovered that the human body has an efficient appetite control centre of its own. Dr Davis took a group of newly weaned infants and allowed them to choose their own food without any outside guidance whatsoever. The results were staggering. She found that without any prompting the infants chose good, varied diets. They ate the right types of food in the correct quantities and their growth rates, development and appearance were all just as satisfactory as those of babies who had been eating foods chosen by experts.

More recently other researchers have found that there is a natural tranquillizer in the human brain and that a pain killer, as powerful and as effective as morphine, is released when pain needs to be overruled. It has been shown, too, that when a person with an infection develops a mild temperature and loses his appetite, both symptoms are signs that the body is dealing with the infection itself. The sort of bugs that commonly produce infections need regular, fresh food supplies – and they can't cope with heat. When you lose your appetite and your temperature goes up, the infection-producing organisms will be threatened and weakened.

A few years ago I wrote a book called *Bodypower* which contained a comprehensive account of the human body's remarkable self-healing mechanisms. The evidence is unquestionable, but it is significant that it has been ignored and even positively suppressed by members of the medical profession. Ruled and still convinced by the mechanistic philosophy of Descartes, modern members of the profession have been strangely reluctant to acknowledge the importance of these discoveries. They have found it easier to believe that they, and they alone, have the answers to all health problems than to accept that they must work together with the body's own self-healing systems to obtain the maximum benefit with the minimum of disruption.

Members of the medical establishment, and in particular doctors involved in medical education, have been slow to accept that the mechanistic philosophy could possibly be wrong. When, almost a decade ago, I wrote a newspaper article suggesting that high blood pressure was a natural response to stress and pressure and that it could sometimes be alleviated by learning to relax, a professor at one of Britain's medical schools wrote to the editor to complain and announced that if I had expressed such ideas as a student of his I would never have been allowed to qualify. (Today, of course, even reactionary professors will admit that stress and high blood pressure are closely linked.)

To a certain extent this repressive and somewhat depressing attitude is understandable. After all, when Descartes first put forward his mechanistic philosophy, doctors had very little to offer in the way of science. They relied on black magic and faith and had to work hard to create the myth that they were alone in knowing the secrets of good health.

And so, despite the evidence that now exists to show the extent of the body's own healing powers, large numbers of the medical profession persist with the mechanistic philosophy. And it is hardly surprising that since they argue that the body is a machine, they also claim that the best person to deal with any problems is a mechanic – a doctor.

A second reason why natural healing mechanisms have not been accepted is that there are today many commercial interests and pressure groups which have a vested interest in maintaining the status quo and protecting and preserving the traditional attitudes towards health and healing.

The paternalistic approach towards medicine suits industry well. The drugs industry, for example, which would suffer badly if the mechanistic approach towards medical care was revised, makes many millions of pounds every year out of the fact that doctors prescribe huge quantities of drugs. Over the years the drugs industry has seen to it that there are many powerful links between the industry and the medical profession. No secret is made of the fact that if the industry were to suffer in any way, the profession would suffer too. A weakening of the international drugs industry would see the end to the existence of the majority of medical journals, an end to free trips abroad to conferences and symposia, an end to many research grants, an end to company sponsorship of medical events and, perhaps most important of all, an end to the drugs industry's ability to protect the medical profession. It is a neat circle of interdependence.

The result is that a large number of practising doctors still claim that all symptoms require interventionist treatment of some kind and that the majority of disorders are best treated by suppressing the body's own responses. They know only too well that if they were to accept that diseases such as high blood pressure or insomnia could be treated effectively without drug therapy, both the industry and the medical profession would suffer enormously.

This unhealthy obsession with drugs has damaged the medical profession. Not only has the obsession meant that doctors have remained blind to the potential benefits of the body's variety of self-healing systems, it has also resulted in a

15

tremendous increase in the number of patients being injured by medical treatment. The fact is that if there are ten patients lying in a hospital ward today, then the chances are that one of them is there because he has been made ill by doctors. Or, to put the same thing in a different way, if you develop fresh symptoms after being treated by your doctor, the chances are that your new symptoms were caused by the treatment given to you for your original problem. Although it is often patients who are blamed for expecting too many wonder pills, it is doctors addicted to prescribing who create the problem in the first place.

Drugs of one sort or another have undoubtedly played a major part in the development of twentieth-century society. Penicillin alone has saved thousands of lives. The contraceptive pill has saved society from an overpopulation explosion. Insulin has helped millions of diabetics live normal, healthy, comfortable lives. Steroids have revolutionized treatments for conditions such as asthma and arthritis.

But drugs have not been used wisely or cautiously. Despite the available evidence that drugs which can cure also kill, doctors have consistently obeyed drug company exhortations to keep on prescribing. A quarter of a century ago doctors wrote about four prescriptions a year for each of their patients. These days they write out 6.5 prescriptions a year for their patients. And the figure is rising. Although the number of doctor–patient consultations has fallen in the last twenty-five years, the number of prescriptions written per person per year has gone up dramatically.

Doctors frequently claim that they write out all these prescriptions because patients demand drugs. That simply isn't true. Roughly one half of all the drugs prescribed are never used at all, but simply end up in bathroom cabinets, discolouring and gathering dust. The truth is that doctors have been pushed and bullied into overprescribing and now overprescribe out of habit and addiction rather than to satisfy the demands of their patients.

Not that it is just in the quantity of drugs they prescribe that doctors are at fault. They also prescribe far too many different drugs. In 1977 the World Health Organization asked a group of experts to decide which drugs – out of the many thousands now on the market – were really necessary. The expert

16

committee came to the rather surprising conclusion that doctors ought to be able to deal with most health problems (including all tropical diseases) with a library of no more than two hundred drugs and vaccines. Since 1977 the expert committee has reconsidered its list twice but has made only minor adjustments.

Despite this, doctors throughout the Western world continue to prescribe drugs that are inappropriate, unnecessary, dangerous or ineffective. Misled by drug company advertising, they continue to prescribe drugs that have been recognized as dangerous and they overuse drugs that are in themselves safe and useful.

One major problem is undoubtedly the appallingly low standard of teaching in medical schools. Academics are often more concerned with their own research projects than with the students they are paid to teach. The result is that out-of-date philosophies and techniques are handed on to generation after generation. Graduates know far too little about the drugs they will spend their lives prescribing.

Speaking at a symposium held at the Royal Society of Medicine in London in 1983, British physician Professor Lant pointed out that 50 per cent of the prescriptions written for antibiotics were either not necessary or inappropriate. According to Professor Lawson of the Royal Infirmary in Glasgow, drug treatment side-effects occur in no less than 25 per cent of patients on medical wards. This sort of prescribing anarchy suggests a high level of dangerous incompetence.

The group of drugs which best illustrates the zealous promotional activities of the drug industry and the poor prescribing habits of the medical profession is the so-called minor tranquillizers. In the quarter of a century since they were first introduced, tranquillizers such as Valium and Librium became so widely used that during any one twelve-month period between one in five and one in three women received a prescription for a tranquillizer. In 1981 the health services of sixty-seven of the world's poorest countries spent less on health care than the rich countries spent on tranquillizers. By the time they are eighteen months old some 25 per cent of all babies will have already received a sedative of one sort or another.

In Britain alone there are well over a million people who

have been taking tranquillizers for several years and a quarter of a million people who have been taking them for seven years or more. Since tranquillizers of this sort were never intended to be prescribed for more than a week or two, that rather suggests that there are many doctors who don't know what they are doing.

There are several reasons why all this happened. The first and probably most important reason is that most of the doctors now in practice qualified before drugs of this type appeared on the market. And because post-graduate medical education of any real value is almost non-existent, these doctors got their information about these drugs from the companies making them. If doctors had been prepared to read through all the independent medical literature before prescribing drugs such as Valium in such huge quantities, they would have discovered evidence over ten years ago to show that products of this type could produce aggression, anxiety and sleeplessness. And within a year or two of their being put on the market there was evidence available which proved that these drugs were addictive.

Another reason why so many doctors overprescribe tranquillizers is that they simply don't know what else to do for the vast number of patients requiring help with problems caused or made worse by stress and anxiety.

It was not until the 1960s that it became clear that there was a close link between stress and physical and mental disease. Patients learned about this link at about the same time as doctors. And since traditional medical school training has been largely concerned with purely physical problems, such as heart disease and broken bones, hardly any practising doctors knew what to do with these stress-related symptoms. Today, even though they know that tranquillizers cause problems, doctors continue to prescribe the drugs because they don't know what else to do and they aren't prepared to admit it. The average doctor today has to keep on prescribing tranquillizers because he can see no alternative way of getting through his daily work load.

There is an alternative, of course. If only the medical establishment had not become so dedicated to the mechanistic theory of the human body and so closely dependent on the drugs industry, the medical schools could have been teaching doctors better ways to help patients suffering from anxiety and other stress-related diseases long before tranquillizers became popular.

The drugs industry solution only succeeded because the medical profession's leaders looked inside the established therapeutic system for all its solutions, rather than being prepared to look outside for fresh, alternative answers. Not that the drugs industry influence has been confined to general practice. The industry has had a major effect on hospital prescribing too. Many of the most widely prescribed heart drugs are neither particularly useful nor especially safe and yet the companies making them promote them with tremendous enthusiasm. And they promote new products for the treatment of disorders such as arthritis with unfaltering optimism.

The cost of all this is, of course, phenomenal. The World Health Organization has estimated that the drug needs of each individual patient should cost no more than one dollar a year. In Britain, and most other developed countries, the amount spent is nearer twenty times that amount. Thanks to doctors' poor education, the international drugs industry continues to make enormously healthy profits. Every time an attempt is made to control prescribing, doctors' representatives (encouraged by the drugs industry, of course) shout loudly about prescribing freedoms and patients rights. The truth is that in Britain alone something like £1,000 million a year could be cut off the National Health Service budget without any patient suffering at all.

And it isn't only the drugs industry which influences medical practices. These days there is a host of companies selling a wide range of expensive gadgets and high technology products. The average piece of equipment has a plug on one end of it, a computer somewhere in the middle and a price tag for thousands of pounds at the other end.

To the uninitiated, high technology medicine may sound as if it has all the answers, but it is truly a Faustian bargain. When you look at scanners, for example, it quickly becomes clear that these may be successful in technical terms, but they are neither successful nor particularly useful in human terms. Such medical toys may make profits for the companies making them and satisfy the pride and professional curiosity of the doctors using them, but they don't save many lives and they certainly don't improve the quality of life for patients. If you look through the medical literature, you will find no evidence to show that CAT scanners are worth buying; yet dozens of hospital doctors have helped organize fund-raising committees to buy themselves the medical equivalent of a bigger, brighter motor car.

There is one final commercial factor that has an influence on the ways that doctors practise medicine: the drive to make money. This influence is best seen at work among our surgeons who have for decades now been so driven by the need to make money that they have done thousands of unnecessary operations simply to enlarge their own bank balances. Even in Britain, where the majority of patients are seen through the National Health Service, countless unnecessary operations are performed every year.

In 1982 Sir George Godber, chief medical officer at the Department of Health and Social Security, wrote that, 'It is commonly believed that many of the 90,000 tonsillectomies done in England and Wales are of questionable benefit.' Why are they done? Well, many of the patients having tonsillectomies are operated on privately. Others are put on to health service lists in order to keep those waiting times as long as possible. People do not want private operations unless the health service list is a long one.

If you think that sounds cynical, consider another popular operation that brings in a good income for many surgeons and which is also done far more often than is necessary: the operation performed for the treatment of patients with peptic ulceration. I would argue that many of the patients with this particular problem would benefit from a solution taken from outside the traditional, narrow avenue of possibilities. But here there is evidence to show that surgeons have the choice of a safer, non-surgical alternative which they prefer to ignore for their own commercial reasons. There is, in fact, a drug available (cimetidine) which, as studies indicate, heals 75 per cent of duodenal ulcers in four weeks and a further 10 per cent in eight weeks. It has been estimated that the number of operations could easily be cut by up to a half.

Apart from Cartesian philosophy, there is another, much older tradition which has also played an important part in regulating medical practice for many centuries. And that is that the relationship between the doctor and the patient has been based on a sale of information, advice and skill.

If a patient falls ill, he visits a doctor, receives advice and treatment, pays a fee and either gets better or comes back again. This simple and well-established tradition has had a dominating effect on medical thought. It has also prevented doctors from accepting the idea of preventive medicine.

Taking more of an interest in preventive medicine would have hardly destroyed the mechanistic philosophy or taken doctors very far along the road towards considering the genuine possibilities offered by the self-healing philosophy, but it would have been a start. If doctors had been prepared to put effort and enthusiasm into understanding their patients' lifestyles and into encouraging them to change their more dangerous activities, they would at least have gone some of the way towards persuading their patients to take back some of the responsibility for their own health.

It isn't as though preventive medicine is a new concept. After all, Hippocrates argued at length that the relationship between a man and his environment is an important one. He pointed out that the health of an individual depends to a very large extent on his personal habits and the world he lives in. He believed that understanding and influencing a man's environment is an essential way of keeping him healthy.

Over the centuries since Hippocrates spelt out the importance of preventive medicine other experts have shown that in order to be effective doctors must take into account four different aspects of each patient's life. First, they must consider his general environment: the air he breathes, the water he drinks, and the general climate of the country he lives in. All these factors must inevitably have an influence on his health. The man who lives in the jungle and drinks contaminated water from stagnant pools will suffer different problems from the man who lives in New York State or Paris.

Second, they must consider his immediate environment. The man who lives in a mansion standing in thirty acres of his own land will be subject to different pressures from the man living in a small two-room apartment. And the man whose job consists of sitting behind a desk will suffer different problems from the man who spends his days driving a bus.

21

Third, the patient's personal environment must be considered. Smoking, eating and drinking habits will all influence a man's health and all have an effect on the type of illnesses from which he suffers. Finally, if a man is to be protected effectively, his doctor must know what sort of person he is. An individual's personality will have a powerful effect on the way that he responds to his immediate environment. It will, of course, also have an important effect on the way he gets on with the people around him – including the doctor.

Today a large number of doctors agree that attempting to treat patients without investigating their environment is like trying to grow seeds without looking at the soil you're trying to grow them in. Indeed, it is by no means going too far to say that treating a patient with drugs or surgery without investigating his personality or outside environment is rather like pulling a plant that isn't growing properly out of its pot, nibbling at its roots with secateurs and then putting it straight back into the same pot-full of soil.

But despite all the evidence showing the value of preventive medicine, the medical profession has continued to toy with the idea rather unenthusiastically. History contains a thousand lessons to show that doctors can do a tremendous amount of good simply by advising their patients about their lifestyle.

Modern, twentieth-century doctors have persistently failed to make the best of the opportunities they have had. They have made two basic errors in the way that they have tried to use the principles of preventive medicine. In the first place they have tried to turn preventive medicine into a new medical speciality involving patients and doctors in a traditional one-to-one relationship. It is easy to understand just how this approach became popular with doctors. It does, after all, turn preventive medicine into a fairly ordinary commercial process with the doctor getting paid a specific fee and retaining all the responsibility. The patient has no added responsibility for his own health apart from remembering to turn up at the surgery or clinic for a 'check-up' or consultation.

This new version of preventive medicine now appears in many different forms. So, for example, you can visit your doctor and have a 'flu jab to stop you getting 'flu. (In fact, there is absolutely no evidence to show that there is any real value in a 'flu jab since the number of 'flu viruses multiplies every year and the chances of your vaccination protecting you against all the right viruses is slim indeed.) Or you can visit your doctor to have your blood pressure checked. (No one has as yet decided which levels of blood pressure are dangerous and need treating and which are safe to leave alone.)

If you are a woman, you can visit your doctor and have a cervical smear done. First introduced about thirty years ago, this test had become so common by 1973 that nearly 50 per cent of all American women over the age of seventeen had had at least one smear during the previous twelve-month period. Unfortunately, however, the cervical smear was accepted as a diagnostic tool long before proper tests on its validity had been done. Today, after millions of smears have been taken, there is still confusion about which women should have smears done, at what age smears are most useful and which women are most at risk. It is widely accepted that the cost of providing all women with annual smears would be prohibitively expensive and yet if annual smears aren't done, tumours which grow quickly (and those are the ones which need to be picked up early) aren't picked up soon enough.

Astonishingly, there still isn't any real evidence to show that cancer smear campaigns have been responsible for any appreciable fall in the incident of cervical cancer. But there is plenty of evidence to show that different cytologists reading the same slides often produce different reports. And there is also plenty of evidence to show that many thousands of women have been worried into illness by being told that they need to have follow-up smears performed for 'technical' reasons.

The other main innovation offered by doctors as a type of preventive medicine has been the annual 'check-up' or general medical screening examination. Check-ups and screening examinations do, in fact, go back to the early part of the twentieth century. As long ago as 1917 more than 10 per cent of the 300 largest American corporations were sponsoring regular examinations of their employees. When over half of 4 million draftees called up during the First World War were found to be either completely or partly unfit for military service, insurance companies became enthusiastic about the idea of screening the general population too.

Today screening clinics are booming. And yet there still isn't any real evidence to suggest that health checks do any good. Indeed, one recent study financed by the British government has concluded that regular screening examinations are both expensive and ineffective. When two groups of individuals were compared, it was found that there was no significant difference between the health of those individuals who had been regularly screened throughout a seven-year period and those individuals who had not been screened. A study of 7,000 patients showed that those who had had health checks were no more or less likely to lose time from work, to need admitting to hospital, to have a visit from their family doctor, or to die any sooner than those who hadn't had health checks.

Similar results have come from surveys conducted in other countries. In Canada a task force studied the question of medical screening for three years before coming to the conclusion that annual check-ups should be abandoned since they were both inefficient and potentially harmful. (Check-ups tend to give patients a false sense of confidence and to encourage them to ignore subsequent warning signs or symptoms. The problem, in short, is that the screening takes away even more personal responsibility from the patient and hands it to his physician.)

The second mistake that doctors have made in trying to introduce preventive medicine into the community in a professionally acceptable way is to do so publicly without first coming to some agreement among themselves and without taking care to silence the commercial groups and lobbyists which have a vested interest in fighting for specific products and types of products. The result has been chaos and confusion. And, sadly, a diminution in the ability of the medical profession as a whole to attract attention when speaking on any important issue.

Take the world of food, for example. There is an enormous amount of controversy here. Should you eat salt? How much fibre should you eat? Are animal fats good for you or bad for you? If you listen carefully to everything the so-called experts have to say, you'll end up thoroughly confused because while one group will tell you one thing, another equally eminent group will say exactly the opposite.

It's not difficult to understand how this happens. Imagine, for example, that a lone researcher in Sweden produces a piece

24

oversold itself. It had promised far more than it could offer. As a result, many millions of patients who had put all their trust in their doctors had had their trust shattered when they had fallen ill. They had been promised good health and longevity and their doctors had been unable to fulfil either promise.

Second, it had put far too much pressure on doctors themselves. For some time now doctors have been found to be the unhealthiest group of individuals in the world. They die younger than most other people. They commit suicide more often. They have more heart disease and more peptic ulcerations. They need psychiatric advice more often than most other groups. They turn to alcohol and drugs far more frequently that most of their contemporaries. Their marriages do not survive. They crumble and they shatter under the tremendous pressure. They have put themselves into an impossible situation. How can they pretend to promise the rest of the world good health when their own state of health is so terrible? Who would trust a bankrupt accountant, a car mechanic reduced to thumbing a lift, a dietitian with a weight problem or a lawyer behind bars?

Third, by denying their patients a chance to take back more personal responsibility for their own health, twentieth-century doctors have failed to take advantage of the rapidly growing amount of evidence pointing to the powerful self-healing qualities of the human body – self-healing techniques which cost nothing, are free of side-effects and offer protection as well as cure, well-being as well as good health.

Finally, and most important of all, twentieth-century doctors have, by strengthening the mechanistic philosophy of health, denied each one of us the opportunity to experience and benefit from the remarkable self-healing powers hidden within our own minds. And by denying us the chance to learn how to utilize our 'mindpower', doctors have ignored a healing process which is far more powerful than the body's own automatic healing processes. It is a hidden force of remarkable depth and exceptional strength. It is to natural self-healing as a shout is to a whisper.

of evidence showing that runner beans cause migraine. Now, because food and health are always of interest some newspaper or television correspondent will notice this research work and will print a paragraph or two detailing the results. At this point little harm will have been done. The research work will have affected relatively few people.

But by now the Runner Bean Marketing Board will have been alerted. Its advisers will scour the world's literature until they find an expert prepared to argue that runner beans are good for you. They may, if they are lucky, find a researcher in, say, Australia or California, who believes that without daily runner beans we run an increased risk of developing liver disease.

Frightened that the consumption of runner beans might be damaged by the original Swedish report, the Runner Bean Marketing Board (which is, of course, financed by the farmers whose livelihood depends upon the steady marketing and sale of runner beans) will pay for the foreign research scientist to go on an international tour. They'll arrange for him to hold press conferences and they'll send copies of his report to doctors and dietitians everywhere.

At this point the Broad Bean Marketing Board will get worried. They will see all this publicity for runner beans as a threat and will look around for an expert or two of their own. They'll come up with a specialist in Germany or Israel who believes that broad beans prevent heart disease or tooth decay. They'll provide him with an international platform from which to expound his views. And they won't be particularly worried if he also uses the massive publicity machine with which they have armed him to propound another dotty theory that carrots cause baldness and impotence. After all, their reasoning will go, if people stop buying carrots, they'll probably buy more broad beans.

The Carrot Marketing Board won't be too pleased by this new development, however, and they'll quickly launch a campaign of their own. In no time at all hundreds of experts from all around the world will be arguing with one another, producing quite different statistics, making all sorts of outrageous claims and ensuring that no one listens to anything that doctors say.

The food industry was one of the first to realize that you can buy any number of medical experts for a few grants and a fistful of airline tickets to conferences in Miami. And it has become one of the most successful industries at lobbying.

To give a more specific example, consider animal fat. The way in which our understanding of the importance of animal fat has been confused highlights the power, effectiveness and consequences of this type of enthusiastic commercial lobbying. Animal fat is the one foodstuff that most of the genuinely independent experts agree we really should avoid if we want to stay healthy. In 1953 it was shown that there was a convincing correlation between a high intake of animal fat and the development of heart disease.

In 1982 the World Health Organization, which always takes its time before coming to any conclusion, published a recommendation of its own advising people to cut down on fat. Numerous major scientific and medical committees around the world have agreed that we should eat less fatty meat, less butter, less cream and fewer eggs.

Look at the evidence coolly and scientifically and there isn't much doubt about it. And in many countries around the world a reduction in the consumption of animal fat has led to a reduction in the incidence of heart disease.

In Britain, however, confusion and chaos have remained. The consumption of animal fat has remained high. And the incidence of heart disease has not fallen. I think that the credit (if that is the right word) for this failure by British doctors to convince people to eat less fat must be shared by Britain's farmers and food manufacturers, who have between them organized a powerful and effective lobby to disguise the truth about animal fats. Since they have an obvious commercial interest in ensuring that we continue to eat lots of butter and drink plenty of milk British farmers and food manufacturers have joined together to pay for a number of extremely effective propaganda organizations. These organizations do their work in a number of ways

First, they bombard journalists of all kinds with information suggesting that animal fats really aren't bad for you after all. That ensures a certain amount of confusion in the press and on television. Then, they send doctors a stream of information prepared by their own team of hired experts. I keep up-to-date files on all medical subjects and before writing

26

this page I took out my file on fats and weighed the papers collected. The accumulated papers and reports weighed 7½ Of that, about 7 lbs had been written, published or inspired such partisan organizations as the Butter Informat Council. When these techniques fail they will try ot methods.

In response the medical profession has become more more aggressive, dominating and dogmatic. Doctors h failed to put advice into perspective and they have been dra into long, complicated arguments by lobbyists anxious produce as much confusion as possible. What started as attempt to offer useful and practical advice on how to s healthy has become something quite different, for instead offering information doctors have once more started to g instructions.

Once again the result has been that the freedom of individual patient has been eroded. The medical professio flirtations with preventive medicine have failed to give peo more responsibility for their own health and have failed to le doctors towards the principles of self-healing. Paradoxica and unexpectedly the doctors' attempts to utilize the princip of preventive medicine have strengthened the traditior medical philosophy which rules that the doctor shou dominate and make all the decisions while the patient shou listen and obey.

By a combination of accident and design the twentie century has see the traditionally dominant role of the doct confirmed and strengthened and the traditionally subservie role of the patient confirmed equally vehemently. To a certa extent patients have encouraged this trend. When you a frightened and ill, it is comforting to have someone who ca take over your life for you. When you are anxious and worri about your health, it is reassuring to be able to hand over a responsibility to a dispassionate professional. But as I studie the contrasting roles of patients and doctors in the la twentieth century, it became clear to me that the relationsh had become unhealthy. Patients had been encouraged to har over too much responsibility. This unequal and unbalance distribution of responsibility had had a number of bad effect First, it had undoubtedly damaged the relationship betwee doctors and patients. The medical profession had, in the en

27

CHAPTER 3

The role of the healer and the role of the patient

The late 1970s and early 1980s were for me confusing, bewildering years. Convinced that the medical profession's full-blooded support for an entirely mechanistic approach to health care was wrong, I resigned from my medical practice to spend my time writing about medicine and searching for a more practical solution that would enable doctors and patients to work together.

I had become disillusioned with the way that orthodox medicine is practised for a good many reasons. But the most important reason was that I felt that it was quite wrong for doctors to regard medical care as an exclusive science. Nearly all the doctors I knew were caring, considerate individuals. They desperately wanted to help their patients get better and they worried about them endlessly when they didn't. But they had all been trained to regard themselves as offering a complete, caring package. They had been taught to take over total responsibility for the health of each patient they saw. And most of them seemed to feel uncomfortable when their authority was threatened in any way.

So, for example, I remember a consultant with whom I worked as a young hospital doctor becoming quite red with rage when a patient told him that she had visited an osteopath. As far as the hospital consultant was concerned, the patient had betrayed him in a treacherous way. He firmly believed that she had, by seeking advice from another professional, deliberately sought to humiliate him. And that consultant was by no means the exception. Indeed, from my experience as a doctor in hospital and in general practice I would say that the

29

consultant's reaction was a fairly standard one.

Nor is it just when their patients see unorthodox practitioners that doctors get upset. Within the last ten years I have met many doctors who have been so proprietorial about their patients that they have felt aggrieved if their patients have dared even to talk to other medical men.

One general practitioner I knew would refuse to see patients ever again if they were brave enough to ask for second opinions from other doctors. As far as he was concerned, the patient's health belonged to the doctor looking after him and the patient had no right at all to look elsewhere for advice or treatment.

This particular doctor's attitude caused many patients deep unhappiness. I remember one young patient, whom I shall call Karen, whose life was deeply influenced by the doctor's sense of ownership. Karen worked in a hairdressing salon and had a boyfriend who was unemployed but struggling to start a small business as a photographer. She was nineteen and he was a year older, and they were sleeping together.

For the first few weeks of their courtship they used no contraceptive precautions, but then a scary few days waiting for a delayed menstrual period sent Karen running along to her general practitioner to ask for help. She wanted to start taking the contraceptive pill and as a young, fit, healthy girl with no personal or family history likely to cause problems there were no medical reasons why she shouldn't have been given a prescription for the first month's pills there and then.

Karen's doctor was, however, a staunch Catholic and he refused to give Karen a prescription. He told her that he did not approve of contraception and would not in any circumstances be prepared to write out a prescription for any contraceptive pills. And not only did he allow his personal moral beliefs to decide what Karen could or could not do with her body, but he also told her that he would remove her name from his list of patients if he found out that she had obtained the pill from any other doctor. He made it fairly clear that her parents would be left in no doubt as to the cause of this medical excommunication. By the time Karen changed doctors she was six months pregnant. And the course of her life had been changed irrevocably by the proprietorial attitude of her family general practitioner.

I could relate dozens of similar stories to illustrate this same point, but I'll confine myself to just one more. This time I'll call the patient Mary, although that was not her name. She was twenty-two and very pretty. But she had one problem that worried her enormously: the size of her breasts. She was so well endowed by nature that her breasts had dominated her life and had, in particular, dominated her relationships with men. From the age of twelve or thirteen she had been subjected to all sorts of lewd remarks from strangers as well as friends, and she had, not unnaturally, become extremely self-conscious about her size. She wanted to have a plastic surgery operation and have the size of her breasts reduced.

Her doctor laughed at her when she told him what she wanted. He told her that most young women would have been delighted with breasts of such a size. He told her that he thought it would be a crying shame to have them reduced and that he wouldn't even allow her to contemplate such butchery. He told her that she should go away and enjoy herself and be grateful for her full and voluptuous figure.

She went away but she didn't enjoy herself and she didn't manage to feel grateful for having such a full and voluptuous figure. She still felt dominated by her breasts and still wanted to have them reduced in size by a surgeon. And so she answered an advertisement she found in a magazine and visited a private clinic.

It took her nearly a year to save up for the operation and it was an absolute disaster. The surgeon was crude and clumsy and she was discharged from the clinic with breasts that were mis-shapen, still bleeding and painful rather than just tender. Back home in her flat she couldn't stand the pain and so she dragged herself to her doctor's evening surgery.

It is difficult to describe the doctor's conduct, but to say that he was unsympathetic is an understatement. He berated her for her stupidity in visiting a private clinic. He shouted at her for allowing herself to be disfigured. He told her off for disobeying his instructions and having her breasts reduced in size. And then he told her that because she had visited another doctor without his permission he would not be prepared to provide her with any treatment nor to see her again. The one thing he couldn't find himself to forgive was that she had dared to go behind his back and see another doctor. She had been unfaithful to him and shared her body with another.

I have even known doctors get upset because patients have dared to treat themselves. Now, under some circumstances, this is understandable. If a doctor is giving a patient pills for a heart condition and that patient then goes away from the surgery and buys an over-the-counter remedy, there is a very real danger that the two drugs will interact badly. But, under other circumstances, it is less easy to explain why the doctor gets so upset.

For several years now I have frequently encouraged patients suffering from insomnia to try and deal with their problem without the aid of sleeping pills My argument is that sleeping pills do not provide a long-term answer; they merely provide a short-term solution. And I believe that my argument is strengthened by the fact that when they have been used for more than a week or two sleeping pills stop helping people get to sleep and start keeping them awake. Even the companies which make sleeping tablets usually suggest that their products are best used as occasional aids.

But after giving this advice on radio programmes, I have on several occasions spoken to patients who have told me that they wouldn't dare try other solutions or try stopping their sleeping pills because their doctors would be offended. One patient rang me up in tears to tell me that when she had told her doctor that she could manage without sleeping pills he had shouted at her. He had been offended because she had been able to overcome her problem without his help and no longer needed regular prescriptions from him.

That sort of incident is by no means unusual. The same sort of thing has happened quite frequently with patients taking tranquillizers. All this seemed to me to be quite wrong. At that stage I began to look towards alternative medicine as a possible solution.

During the 1970s I was by no means the only person becoming disenchanted with the attitudes of orthodox medical practitioners. Huge numbers of patients had turned away from registered medical practitioners and were seeking help from alternative or complementary medical practitioners.

And during that time the number of people seeking help from acupuncturists, homoeopaths, hypnotherapists, osteopaths and others was rising rapidly. In 1981 a third of the French population tried unorthodox types of medicine. By 1983 the number of people in Britain seeking help from alternative practitioners had reached one million for the first time and was said to be rising at a quite extraordinary rate. In 1984 a British survey showed that one out of every three people had used alternative practitioners. In America, Germany, Australia, Scandinavia and just about every other developed country the picture was very similar.

People started consulting alternative medical practitioners for many different reasons. Some turned away from orthodox, registered medical practitioners because they wanted more control over their own health and they felt that they would be allowed to share control if they visited alternative practitioners. Some were frightened by the high incidence of side-effects associated with modern drugs and surgical techniques. Others visited alternative practitioners simply because they had failed to find either relief or cure from orthodox medicine.

As a scientifically trained sceptic, I found many of the claims made by alternative practitioners puzzling. I found a few of them downright dishonest. But some of the better established alternative remedies seemed to me to offer sound, logical explanations for the cures they promised. Acupuncture, for example, seemed to me to be useful and effective. When I looked through scientific journals published around the world I found a good deal of evidence to show that the claims made by skilful acupuncturists were reasonable and sound. In 1974, for example, four American surgeons reported that they had treated over 300 patients in and around the New York area by acupuncture. The surgeons stated that in over three quarters of the cases they had found that acupuncture is one of the most effective treatments available for arthritis, neuralgia and other skeletomuscular pains.

Two doctors writing in the Canadian Anaesthetists Society Journal in the same year wrote that, 'reports of a large number of surgical cases operated on under acupuncture anaesthesia with a success rate of up to 90 per cent have now been sufficiently substantiated that the effectiveness of acupuncture can no longer be doubted.'

By 1979 so much had been published about acupuncture and it had been so widely tested and tried that at a meeting of medical representatives from all six of the World Health Organization's regions it was concluded that 'the sheer weight of evidence demands that it must be taken seriously as a clinical procedure of considerable value.'

More recently the World Health Organization actually condemned doctors for failing to accept acupuncture as a useful medical technique, arguing that the antagonistic attitude of many doctors and other health professions is proving a major obstacle hindering the acceptance of acupuncture.

But the more I looked at the alternative remedies, the more I decided that, although some seemed sensible and some seemed silly, not one could be seen as a genuinely complete alternative to orthodox medicine. That seemed to me to be a great weakness.

The more useful and the more responsible an alternative practitioner was, the more he would insist that he offered not a complete but a partial alternative to orthodox medicine. The best qualified alternative practitioners all told me that they saw themselves as offering a complementary service to orthodox medicine. The best acupuncturists, hypnotherapists and osteopaths all worked alongside registered medical practitioners rather than competing with them.

Only the dottiest and least responsible alternative practitioners claimed to offer a complete service. The sensible ones all admitted that they always sent some of their patients to see general practitioners or hospital specialists. They agreed that they didn't deal with heart attack victims or patients with compound fractures or brain haemorrhages. It seemed to me that none of these so-called alternative forms of medicine were really 'alternatives' at all. They were, rather, variations on an existing theme.

Indeed, by the early 1980s there were huge numbers of orthodox doctors already practising some of the so-called alternative remedies. There were doctors practising hypnotherapy, osteopathy, homoeopathy and acupuncture, for example. Admittedly, many of them were badly trained and offering a woefully inadequate service. But they had had very little difficulty in accommodating these strange new disciplines into their own medical practices. Even the British Medical Association, the doctor's trade union, had begun to take an interest in alternative medicine and had set up a special committee to investigate alternative medicine.

The so-called alternatives were being drawn into orthodox medicine. Acupuncture and osteopathy were being linked up alongside traditional medical remedies such as drugs and surgery. It seemed perfectly clear to me that within another couple of decades all the very best aspects of alternative medicine would have been incorporated into traditional medical practices. And alternative medical practitioners would be working alongside registered medical practitioners in health centres and clinics all over the country.

There was something else too that convinced me that the new wave of alternative remedies weren't really alternatives at all. And that was that the practitioners of alternative remedies were mostly following the Cartesian mechanistic theory of the human body. It seemed to me that the majority of alternative practitioners had been so brainwashed by traditional medical thinking, so contaminated by several hundred years of medical thought, that they had fallen into the trap of selling their skills and their products in exactly the same way as any orthodox doctor sells his skills and his products.

To me there seemed to be very little difference between the practitioner scribbling out a prescription for penicillin or a tranquillizer, the practitioner sticking acupuncture needles into his patients, the practitioner handing over a herbal remedy, the practitioner preparing a homoeopathic remedy, the practitioner offering hypnotherapy or the practitioner dancing among the pile of old bones on the living-room carpet. All these people had one thing in common: they were offering an interventionist approach. They wanted to take responsibility for their patients' health and offer their skills and services to people needing help.

During the early 1980s my suspicions and fears about the growing variety of alternative remedies were substantiated in a number of ways. First, there was the fact that all over the world new teaching schools seemed to have been set up to show people how to practise alternative medicine. It had become big business and diplomas were readily for sale. Many of the people practising alternative medicine had done nothing but spend a weekend on a course. Some had simply done short mail order courses.

Second, many alternative practitioners were boasting of the

35

equipment they had. Computers were popular with many alternative practitioners and all sorts of sophisticated bits and pieces of machinery could be seen in the consulting rooms of the most successful alternative practitioners.

Third, there were a growing number of reports showing that patients had been injured or made ill by alternative medicines. It seemed that alternative practitioners offered solutions that could sometimes be just as dangerous as those of orthodox practitioners.

My unavoidable conclusion was that, despite the huge amount of publicity that had been given to alternative medicine, none of these remedies was truly alternative. Many were valuable additions to orthodox medicine. But that was all.

Having decided that alternative practitioners offer little that is really new, I was to a large extent back where I had started in the late 1970s. I felt convinced that there had to be a simple answer to it all, a new philosophy, a new way of looking at health that could revolutionize our approach to sickness and to doctors. And I thought I was getting close to it. But first I felt that I needed to make clear in my own mind exactly what role I thought the professional ought to play.

So far I've been fairly critical about health care professionals – and in particular about doctors. But I need now to put the criticism in perspective. For however much I may disapprove of the fact that doctors have become far too paternalistic, however much I may want to draw attention to the short-comings of the medical profession and the drugs industry and the growing alternative health care industry, I do not for one moment think that we could manage without any of these people.

Doctors and all the other health care professionals have a vital role to play in maintaining and preserving our health, in dealing with sickness and disease when it becomes threatening and in helping to care for us when we become frail, weak or disabled.

The problem is, I think, a fairly simple one. Up until today the emphasis has been wrong. The doctor has taken over our health care completely and has left us far too little responsibility. In the past the relationship between doctor and patient

36

has been similar to that of teacher and pupil, employer and employee, master and slave.

I believe that the relationship between doctor and patient should not be weighted at all on the side of the doctor. Both doctor and patient should be entitled to make whatever contributions they consider appropriate or possible. But, and this is I think absolutely vital, the patient should always take the dominant role. The doctor, whether he be surgeon, physician or general practitioner, is there to offer technical advice and help. But he should see his role as technical adviser rather than anything else.

With this sort of relationship established, the doctor's responsibilities will be reduced to a manageable level and the patient's responsibilities will be extended in a way which will enable him to take full advantage of his body's many self-healing mechanisms.

By putting an end to this traditional master–slave relationship we will benefit in three very distinct, practical ways. First, patients will have much more freedom. They will be able to consult whichever practitioner they feel might be able to help without having to worry about upsetting any existing relationship. And with the added freedom there will undoubtedly be more honesty. Patients will see their family doctor, their local acupuncturist or their local herbalist. But they will do so openly and honestly. With things the way they are at the moment, patients do consult other professionals, but they invariably keep quiet about it and avoid telling one practitioner what another has suggested. That can be dangerous.

When I was in general practice a young woman came to see me with a long history of high blood pressure. I started to teach her how to relax, advised her to lose weight, helped her learn how to deal with stress more effectively and, because her blood pressure was quite high, gave her a prescription for some pills which I thought should help. But when I saw her a week later her blood pressure was higher rather than lower. Anxious to control the level of her blood pressure I increased the dose of the tablets and asked her to return to see me in another week.

By that time her blood pressure had gone even higher. I'm not quite sure what made me ask her whether she was taking any other treatment – at the time it wasn't a question I asked routinely – but I did. And, after a moment's hesitation she confessed quite tearfully that she had been to a local herbalist and had been taking a remedy the herbalist had recommended. She hadn't told me about it because she'd felt sure that I would be offended. What had happened, of course, was that the two remedies had interacted dangerously, with the result that her high blood pressure, instead of falling, had risen even higher.

By changing the proprietorial attitude of medical professionals, we will free patients to consult whichever professional they like – and to then be honest about what treatments they have tried or are trying. That will be a much safer approach. (In those countries where doctors are paid an annual retainer or capitation fee for looking after patients the system will have to be changed so that doctors receive a fee for each consultation. The capitation fee strengthens the doctor's feeling of ownership.)

The second advantage of putting an end to the paternalistic relationship between doctors and patients will be that the outdated mechanistic approach will be weakened. Doctors find it easy to think of the patient's body as a piece of machinery because they find it easy to think of the patient as an object rather than a person. Doctors frequently talk of patients as 'cases' or 'diseases' rather than as individual people. In hospital a man or woman will frequently become 'the liver in the end bed' or the 'heart attack in the second bed on the right'. Under those circumstances it is hardly surprising that doctors then treat their patients as machines. (It is sometimes quite difficult to decide which comes first: the paternalistic approach or the mechanistic philosophy. But as long as the circle is broken somewhere, it will remain broken.) The third advantage of getting rid of the old-fashioned relationship between doctor and patient is that the doctor will be able to take full advantage of his potential as a healer.

So far I haven't mentioned the role of the doctor as healer, but this is, I think, of absolutely vital importance. Since time immemorial it has been established that doctors, priests, alternative medical professionals, kings, medicine men and all sorts of individuals can have a healing effect on patients simply by being close to them or touching them.

For centuries, for example, there has been a strong belief in the ability of royalty to heal by the laying on of hands. In France healing on a large (and successful) scale was first tried by Clovis the Frank in AD 496. In England this apparently pagan practice is said to have started with Edward the Confessor. Patients would queue for days for a chance to be touched or blessed by a member of the royal family. And they would very often get better as a result of their blessing.

Through the centuries there have been endless examples of the healing effect that doctors can have too. In the Middle Ages, for example, when medicine was in its darkest period and there were few if any useful remedies available to the average practitioner, there were still doctors around who had a remarkably high success rate. If they hadn't had success with at least some of their patients then they wouldn't have stayed in business for long. No one wants to spend money going to see a doctor who never cures any of his patients.

I can still remember vividly one of the first times that I was made aware of the tremendous healing power to which doctors have access simply by virtue of being doctors. A patient of mine called Nan was a regular sufferer from arthritis. Her pains came and went and she used drugs only when absolutely necessary.

One Friday evening she came in late during the surgery and told me that her joints were playing up particularly badly. She desperately needed something to take for the weekend. She also wanted to pick up a prescription for an antibiotic being taken on a long-term basis by her teenage son, who suffered from particularly bad facial acne. I wrote out the two prescriptions, but told her that instead of giving her the usual pain killer I normally prescribed for her I was going to try something new. I wrote out a prescription for a product which had been well tried but which, according to all the evidence I'd read, had a greater chance of producing a lasting improvement. I was very positive about the drug and told her that I thought it could help her a great deal.

When she got to the chemist, the pharmacist only had one of the two drugs in stock. He told her that she would have to wait for the other prescription. She misunderstood what he had told her and thought that the tablets she was taking home were the ones I had prescribed for her arthritis. In fact, they were the ones normally taken by her son the acne-sufferer. She then proceeded to take the antibiotics thinking that they would have a useful effect on her arthritis pains.

39

Remarkably, after two days her arthritis was far less troublesome than it had ever been. She was virtually free of pain and quite able to walk about freely. She was so delighted that she came back to the surgery to tell me the good news. She showed me the bottle of pills she was taking to make sure that I made a note in her medical records of the drug that had proved so efficacious. It was then that I realized that she was taking the wrong drug. The antibiotics could not possibly have had any useful effect on her joint pains. And that was the first practical experience I had of the power of the placebo effect.

At medical school I'd never heard the word 'placebo' mentioned and there certainly had not been any mention of the way that apparently powerless pills can have a useful, practical effect in medical practice. But that experience triggered my interest in the subject and I started hunting through the medical journals for more examples of the effectiveness of this type of healing.

I found that the medical literature was absolutely full of references to placebo power. It had all really started, it seemed, during the Second World War when an American army medical officer had run out of morphine while treating injured soldiers. Rather than admit to the soldiers (many of whom were in terrible pain) that he had nothing to give them the doctor found some vials of plain water and gave those by injection. To his amazement the water proved to be as powerful a pain killer as morphine. The soldiers' pains were eased even though they'd been injected with nothing more powerful than water.

In the years which followed, the power of the placebo was investigated quite thoroughly by many experts. In 1946 a researcher called Jellinek found that out of 199 patients who complained of having a headache, 120 lost their headache when given nothing more powerful than a sugar tablet. It was shown that 30 per cent of patients with severe, steady, post-operative pain got relief from placebos. And according to a report in the *British Medical Journal* in 1970 no less than 60 per cent of patients suffering from angina had fewer attacks when given placebo tablets and told that their attacks would be less frequent.

Further research has shown that although the colour, shape and size of a placebo tablet affects its efficacy, nothing governs the power of a placebo quite so much as the enthusiasm with which it is offered to the patient.

So, if a doctor gives a patient a placebo tablet and says something like, 'Try this it might help you a little', the chances of the placebo working are relatively slight.

If, however, the doctor hands over the placebo tablet with an enthusiastic comment such as, 'Try this. It's the most powerful and effective drug on the market. It will help you', the chances of the placebo working are increased enormously.

It is even possible for doctors to influence the sort of side-effects patients are likely to get – simply by what they say.

So, if a doctor handing over a pill (whether or not it is a placebo pill) says, 'Watch out. This pill may produce a rash and make you feel drowsy', the chances are very high that the patient will complain that the pill makes him feel drowsy and gives him a rash. Our bodies respond, it seems, not simply to what is in a tablet but to what we expect it to contain.

Nor is it just tablets and pills and drugs that operate the placebo effect. We associate the placebo effect with pills simply because we associate doctors with pills, but in fact the placebo effect can work in a thousand other ways too.

So, for example, if a surgeon who is about to operate on a patient says, 'I'm afraid that when you wake up you'll be in a lot of pain and probably rolling around in agony', the patient will probably wake up in a good deal of pain. (That sounds like a silly thing for any surgeon to say but I've known it done.)

Whereas if a surgeon who is about to operate on a patient says something like, 'When you wake up you will feel much better and calmer and we will make sure that you do not suffer any pain', the patient will probably wake up free of pain and discomfort.

To give another example, if a doctor sees a patient who complains of a pain in his neck and says, 'I can help get rid of that pain for you with a little massage', the patient's pain will quite probably disappear after a little massage. It probably won't be the massage that will have got rid of the pain. It will be the fact that the doctor has promised the patient a cure.

By now, of course, it should be fairly clear that if a doctor can have this 'healing' effect, there is nothing at all to stop non-qualified practitioners from producing a similar effect. And that, of course, is just what happens. Many of the alternative practitioners who have a remarkably high degree of success with patients depend very much on the placebo effect. They help their patients get better by being enthusiastic and optimistic.

The ultimate placebo effect is obtained by those practitioners who do not use any tricks or drugs or mechanical aids, but who simply 'heal' their patients either by being close to them or by touching them. I've seen this work, too, and I'm totally convinced that it is possible to 'heal' a patient simply by telling him or her that you are going to heal them.

I have to admit that I remained sceptical about the abilities of healers to produce genuine changes until I interviewed a healer for a Midlands television programme a year or so ago. The healer had written to me claiming to have unusual healing powers and asking me to help assess her skills. At my request she brought with her to the studio a patient who had for years suffered from bad arthritis and who claimed that the healer had helped get rid of her pains. I was perfectly prepared to accept that the woman's pains had disappeared, but less ready to believe that there had been any genuine changes in her condition.

However, my scepticism faded when I obtained the woman's X-rays from her hospital consultant. I found that there had been a definite radiological improvement. The X-rays taken before the patient had been seen by the healer showed definite arthritis. The X-rays taken afterwards showed virtually no arthritis at all. And an expert radiologist, who did not even know that the patient had been seen by a healer, agreed that there had been a definite and apparently un-explained improvement in the patient's condition.

A hundred years ago that sort of healing event would have been described as a miracle. And even these days there are spiritual healers who argue vehemently that when healing occurs it is thanks to the intervention of spirits from some other world. I think that is nonsense. The majority of responsible healers now agree that there is nothing particularly miraculous about what they do; they don't invoke any unworldly aids, they simply assist the body to heal itself.

The fact is that there is now an enormous amount of evidence to show that 'healing' works by producing a positive effect on the body and can be explained in straightforward physiological terms. (Spiritual healers argue that they can 'cure' people at a distance, but the physiological explanation of healing does not exclude so-called 'distance' healing. Nor do I think there is anything particularly unusual about the fact that animals can be healed.) All the healer does is to trigger the body's internal healing responses and enable the body to heal itself.

I started this short section on placebos and healing by suggesting that by putting an end to the paternalistic, master–slave relationship between doctor and patient, the ability of the doctor to function as a healer would be enhanced. I think that the evidence for that lies in the fact that all the very best healers work *with* their patients.

One of the reasons why alternative health care professionals have won so many patients away from orthodox doctors in recent years is that alternative professionals tend to be friendlier and more obviously compassionate. They still follow the old mechanistic philosophy; they are still inter-ventionists, but they are far less paternalistic. Most of them have not yet had time to acquire the aura of dispassionate professionalism that is so typical of orthodox medical practitioners.

And yet most alternative medicine professionals rely very heavily indeed on the placebo response, on their ability to heal and on their ability to trigger a healing response. The doctor who remains aloof and distanced from his patients will achieve a certain amount of healing effect through blind trust and faith. Patients who want to get better will put an enormous amount of trust in those looking after them. But the doctor who can shatter the now traditional barrier between doctor and patient will be far more likely to produce a positive, healing effect. The doctor must learn to have faith in his patient just as the patient is expected to have faith in his doctor. If the power of the healing effect is to be achieved respect and trust need to be shared between both partners.

By exploring the real role that must be filled by the profes-sional 'healer', I have also, inevitably, redefined the role that must be filled by the patient. Up until today the patient has had a secondary role in medical care.

But the change of role that I have outlined in this chapter

means that I am now encouraging the patient to take advantage of the skills offered by the professionals only as and when they are needed. The patient must seek professional advice when he is unsure about how best to treat specific ailments, symptoms or conditions. He must seek expert, technical help when he can no longer cope with symptoms which threaten his comfort or survival. He must always be prepared to ask for support and encouragement when he feels weakened or threatened. He must never be shy about calling in the professionals.

The independent patient who is in control of his own health will know that unexplained changes and alterations in his body which he can neither explain nor deal with effectively need technical advice as soon as possible. He will be closer to medical advice, not further from it. He will be better able to take advantage of the skills and facilities offered by the wide range of twentieth-century health care professionals. He will be able to select the most appropriate source of help from among the wide range of professionals now offering their services.

But at the same time the independent patient will be better equipped to care for himself. By relegating the professionals to an advisory capacity he will have created a vacuum which he himself can fill with his own personal skills and strengths. Now he can take full advantage of a health-enhancing and disease-devastating range of mental powers which have for too long been ignored, misunderstood and suppressed.

Only the independent patient is in a position to take advantage of 'mindpower'. And it is 'mindpower' which offers the solution I have been seeking. I shall explain exactly how your mind rules your body – and how mindpower works – in the next chapter.

CHAPTER 4

The links between mind and body

A few years ago the majority of medical scientists would have laughed at the idea of there being any substantial link between problems in the mind and problems affecting the body. No doctor with any sort of reputation in the profession would have dared to acknowledge that such a link existed.

Less than ten years ago I wrote a book called *Stress Control* in which I put forward the view that nearly all the common twentieth-century diseases are caused or made worse by stress. I argued that stress was the greatest environmental hazard of our time and that doctors should be spending more time helping to manage stress, rather than simply treating symptoms.

Even then many doctors with powerful academic positions laughed at the idea and dismissed it as hypothetical nonsense. They still believed that all diseases had a physical basis. Today, I very much doubt if there is a doctor or reputable medical scientist anywhere in the world who doesn't accept that stress, fear, anxiety, worry, apprehension, pressure, anger and even joy can all cause quite genuine physical responses and very real diseases.

The figures vary from report to report, but at a conservative estimate at least three quarters of all the problems seen by doctors are illnesses which are either completely or partly psychosomatic in origin. If you include all the illnesses not seen by doctors – and that means such problems as headaches, period pains, mild anxiety, sleeplessness, back problems, colds and so on – then the figures will be even greater. After talking at length to experts working in many different areas of medicine I would estimate that between 90 per cent and 95 per cent of all illnesses can be blamed totally or partially on psychological forces. Our minds are killing us.

Consider the common or garden headache, for example. There are some headaches that are caused by injuries and brain tumours, but experts now agree that at least 98 per cent of all headaches are stress- and pressure-related. When under stress we screw up our eyes, we tighten and tense the muscles around our heads – and we get headaches.

Or take indigestion: one of the commonest disorders known to twentieth-century man. It is so common that if five people sit down to dinner, the chances are that afterwards at least one of them will have stomach pains. Occasionally, indigestion may be caused by poor eating habits or by eating the wrong sort of food. But in the vast majority of cases it is caused by anxiety and nervousness.

Even when indigestion seems to be caused by bad eating habits it is often easy to prove that the root cause was stress. When a man hurries his lunch he is probably hurrying because he is under stress. When a man swallows food without chewing, it is probably because he is desperate to get back to the office to see how his latest deal is going. When a woman grabs a sandwich at her desk it is quite possible that she is feeling anxious about her work.

Some of the evidence that is available links stress to particular types of occupation. So, for example, the importance of industrial stress was first recognized in America in 1956 when a machine operator called James Carter cracked up while working on the General Motors production line in Detroit. Mr Carter had what is now commonly known as a nervous breakdown and he sued General Motors, claiming that the stresses of his job had contributed to his breakdown. It was an important law suit, for Carter won and from that day onwards American industry took the relationship between stress and disease very seriously indeed.

Since then researchers all around the world have published work linking specific occupations with specific types of stress-induced disease.

At one time or another trades unions representing doctors, nurses, tax collectors, school teachers, journalists, taxi drivers, airline pilots and air traffic controllers have all claimed that their members are particularly prone to stress. It has even been argued that some occupations can be linked to particular stress-linked diseases. Dr Jack Dunham, a consultant psychologist working with Berkshire County Council and Bath University in England has recently claimed that the type of classroom stress suffered by schoolteachers can cause infertility.

But the truth is that you don't even have to have a job to suffer from a stress-related disorder. Heaps of researchers have now published work showing that unemployment can produce pressure and stress-related illnesses too. That evidence should have put to rest for ever the old myth that the only people likely to suffer from stress are overworked business executives rushing to catch the next plane. In fact, over the last year or two I have found evidence linking stress to just about every type of human situation and endeavour.

There have been many papers published showing that social situations can cause damaging amounts of stress. In a paper presented to the American Psychiatric Association recently one author showed that the immune system of a recently bereaved widow showed a marked reduction in efficiency – stress had changed her body's ability to cope with disease. Another report, published in the Journal of the American Medical Association showed that the type of depression which is suffered following a bereavement can affect the body's internal defence mechanisms so violently that small, cancerous tumours which might have otherwise been suppressed by the body's own defences can survive, grow and eventually kill the patient. A third study, published this time in Australia, showed that these changes in the body's internal immune responses and defences take place within a mere eight weeks of the death of a close relative. In other words, just two months after the death of someone close to us our bodies are so badly damaged by the stress that they become exceptionally vulnerable to cancers and infections of all kinds.

And, of course, as just about any doctor will confirm that's just what happens. One partner dies and within a month or two the second partner, previously apparently fit and healthy, will die too. In one large study it was shown that the death rate among widowed individuals was twelve times the rate among a similar group of individuals who had not been bereaved.

Stress won't appear on the death certificate; nevertheless it is the cause of death.

Similar evidence is available for all sorts of other social pressures too. If you're under pressure at home or your love life is too hectic, your chances of having a heart attack are six times greater than normal. The same is true if you have money worries or problems involving close friends. If you are what is known as 'socially mobile' (moving up the promotion ladder, getting a better job, earning more money, living in a bigger house and so on), that can increase your chances of having a heart attack three or four times.

In all these cases the important factor is stress. It is, without a doubt, the major twentieth-century killer.

Although there is now absolutely no doubt that stress is killing many people, there is still one important question to be answered: why are we so much more susceptible to stress, when we have such well-organized lives? Our ancestors had to worry about getting enough to eat, finding somewhere warm and dry to sleep at night, and staying alive while marauding, wild animals wandered around. Most of us have enough to eat and somewhere to live. We don't have to worry too much about being eaten by wild animals and we have central heating, microwave ovens and the choice of several channels of TV entertainment. Compared to our ancestors we have it easy. And yet we suffer more from stress than any of our ancestors ever did. Why?

The answer is quite simple. Our bodies were not designed for the sort of world in which we live today. They were designed for a world in which fighting and running were useful, practical solutions. They were designed to enable us to cope with physical confrontations with sabre-toothed tigers.

Today we respond in the same way. If we come face to face with a problem, our muscles tighten, our hearts beat faster, our blood pressure goes up, adrenalin surges through our veins and our bodies are put on general alert. We can fight, run, jump and climb with astonishing agility.

The trouble is, however, that today's problems are not quite so simple or as straightforward as they used to be. Instead of finding ourselves face to face with a sabre-toothed tiger, a pack of hungry wolves or an angry boar, we are far more likely to find ourselves having to face unemployment, big gas bills, traffic wardens, parking problems or officious policemen. None of these modern problems is easily solved and none can be dealt with by a faster heartbeat, a higher blood pressure or muscles that have been tensed. Our natural, physiological responses no longer help us to cope effectively or appropriately with our problems.

Faced with threats of any kind our bodies respond in the only way they know how: by preparing for physical action. We have not yet evolved fast enough to have learnt that purely physical responses won't help. The real source of the problem is that we have changed our world far faster than our bodies have been able to adapt. At no other time in the history of the world has there been such a constant progression of ideas. Never before have fashions, themes and attitudes changed quite so rapidly. Never before have expectations and pressures been so enormous.

During the last couple of centuries revolutionary changes in medicine, navigation, printing, agriculture, military techniques, design, transport, industrial methods and communication systems have transformed our world. But our bodies are very much the same as they were ten, twenty or a hundred thousand years ago. It takes many thousands of years for the human body to adapt and we have moved far too quickly for our own good.

It is, sadly, those natural responses which cause the ill effects produced by stress. And the symptoms of stress-induced disease are produced because the problems that cause the responses do not go away but last for hours, days, months and even years.

When a hefty gas bill lands on your door mat your body will respond to the threat in the only way it knows how: your heart will beat faster, your blood pressure will go up, your muscles will become tense and your whole body will be prepared for a fight. Unfortunately, your chances of being able to pay the bill are not increased by such simple physiological changes. And, indeed, the responses are worse than useless. They are damaging. Because the gas bill won't go away in a few minutes. The problem will remain for some considerable time. And for as long as the problem remains so your body will remain on the alert.

Like many people, I've been aware of the significance of stress for many years now. But there has always been something puzzling about stress: the fact that it doesn't seem to affect people in the same way. To illustrate what I mean let me describe two patients I knew when I was in general practice.

When I first met Humphrey he was in his mid-thirties and married with two small children. He worked as an assistant manager in a small grocery shop not far from the surgery. To be honest, I don't think the shop really merited an 'assistant manager', but the owner wanted to give Humphrey a bit of status (largely, I suspect, as an excuse for not giving him a pay rise) and so he had bought Humphrey a white coat and a name label for his lapel.

Humphrey was one of life's sufferers. He was hardly ever away from my surgery. And he was constantly worrying about the pressures in his life. He worried if the shop looked like running out of beans or cat food or tomato sauce. He worried if there were lots of customers waiting to be served. He worried if there weren't any customers. He worried if it was raining in case the bad weather kept the customers away. He worried if the sun was shining in case the customers all went swimming or stayed at home sunbathing. He worried about anything and everything. And he made himself ill.

Humphrey had become a one-man example of what stress can do to you. He had high blood pressure; he had asthma which got much worse when he was worried; he had indigestion which wouldn't go away and which suggested that he might have an early duodenal ulcer; he had a patch of eczema which flared up when he got particularly upset about anything; and he had recurrent diarrhoea at the most difficult times of the year. Eventually he even started getting heart pains. When I left my practice he was a physical wreck. He looked about fifty-five rather than thirty-five. He just couldn't cope with the stress in his life.

And yet by anybody's standards Humphrey really didn't have all that much stress to cope with. His wife was loyal, loving and faithful. He had his own home with a small mortgage. He had a good, secure job with a steady income and little real responsibility. He had two healthy children. He should have been relatively stress-free. But he wasn't. He was a

50

stress victim.

Doreen on the other hand see·ned perfectly capable of coping with any amount of stress. She seemed rocklike and untouchable. She had married early, but her first husband had left her with two small children to bring up. She had worked for a while as a school teacher and then married a local builder, given up work and had another two children. Within three years the builder had gone bankrupt and committed suicide leaving Doreen with a drawer full of bills, no money, no house and four children to look after.

Doreen had not only survived, she had thrived. She had gone back to work and within ten years had become headmistress of a large comprehensive school. Her children were all growing up reasonably well, but one was a diabetic and another had managed to get himself into a certain amount of trouble with the local police.

The pressure Doreen was under at school was only matched by the pressure she was under at home. At school she had over a thousand children to look after and a huge staff of teachers to cope with. She had a board of governors and a management committee and a Parent–Teachers Association. She had strikes, drug problems and teenage pregnancies. At home she had no husband, a huge mortgage and four growing and rather boisterous children of her own to look after.

And yet Doreen never suffered from any stress-related diseases. I only saw her professionally twice – for routine vaccinations.

These two, and many hundreds of other patients, convinced me that although stress is a root cause of most twentieth-century diseases, it isn't actually stress itself that ever kills anyone. True, we all respond to physical pressures and dangers in much the same sort of way. If we all stood face to face with an army of sabre-toothed tigers, our hearts would all beat faster. (Some of us would respond more dramatically than others, but we would all respond in some way to the danger.)

But most twentieth-century pressures are abstract fears, worries, anxieties and suspicions. And it is not what is really happening around us that produces a reaction: it is what we suspect might be happening, it is what we think is likely to happen, it is what we imagine.

51

And that is what gave me the clue that enabled me to create the mindpower philosophy. The damage that is done by twentieth-century stress is done through our minds. It is not what is happening around us that is killing us; it is what we think is happening, it is what we suspect may be the consequences.

Brian works for a large car component manufacturer and has a well paid job with them. He is married and has one son, aged nineteen and away at teacher training college. When I first saw Brian he was lying in bed recovering from a heart attack. He readily confessed that he felt sure that his heart attack had been brought on by the pressure he'd been under. He said that nearly all his pressure was related to his job. When I asked him to explain to me exactly what sort of stresses he had to cope with he thought for a long moment before answering.

'It's difficult to answer that,' he confessed. 'There are so many different pressures it's hard to know where to start. But, to give you an idea,' he went on, 'one of my most important functions is to buy in raw materials. If I don't get the raw materials to the factory on time then we can't make any of our products. That can be very worrying.'

'Why is it worrying?' I asked him.

He looked puzzled.

'I know it's your job to get the materials to the factory,' I explained. 'But why do you worry if it looks as if there is going to be a shortage?'

'Well, for a start my job would be on the line,' said Brian.

'You mean you'd get the sack if a supplier didn't provide what you'd ordered?'

'Well, no, I don't suppose I'd get the sack,' admitted Brian. 'But it wouldn't look very good.'

He thought about it for a minute or two longer.

'I'd feel guilty about it,' he said. 'I'd feel as if I'd let the side down.'

'And what if you did get the sack?' I asked him. 'How terrible would that be?'

'Awful,' Brian said quickly.

'Do you enjoy your work?' I asked him.

'Most of the time.'

'But it does have its dull moments?'

He nodded.

'Is there anything you'd like to do but don't have time to do?'

'Lots of things,' he said. 'I write articles on angling for a magazine. I'd like to turn them into a book one day if I had the time.'

'So you'd have things to do if you lost your job?'

'Oh yes,' he agreed.

'How many bedrooms has your house got?'

Brian looked puzzled. 'Four,' he told me.

'How many do you need?' I asked. 'Really need?'

'One,' said Brian after a moment or two. 'Two, perhaps at the most.'

'When did you buy your house?'

'Twenty years ago.'

'And it's probably worth a lot more than you paid for it?'

Brian nodded and smiled. 'It's worth quite a lot,' he admitted. 'People always say that it's wise to put your money in property and it's true.'

'So if you sold it you could buy somewhere smaller and still be quite well off?'

Brian thought for a moment and then nodded. He was still smiling. 'Yes, I suppose so,' he agreed.

'So getting the sack wouldn't be quite so terrible after all?' I said. 'You could buy somewhere smaller, enjoy life more and write your book on fishing.'

There was silence for a moment. 'It's a thought,' said Brian. 'Do you think that's what I should do?'

'No,' I said quickly. 'I'm not suggesting that you should do anything in particular. All I'm trying to do is point out to you that you probably don't have quite so many stresses in your life as you think you have. In fact, it's the way you've been thinking about your work that has turned daily problems and tasks into stresses.'

And what is true of Brian is, of course, true for the rest of us too. We frequently respond not to the realities of our lives but to what we think are the realities. We respond not to the real pressures that surround us but to the pressures we think are there. The stress that is killing us all exists not in the real world around us but in the world that exists in our heads. By changing our society we have changed the type of pressures we have to face. And because those new pressures are so often abstract and ethereal, we create new stresses and fears out of thin air.

It isn't unemployment that causes heart disease; it is the way we respond to unemployment. It isn't gas bills that cause high blood pressure; it is the way we respond to gas bills. It isn't the heavy traffic and the telephone that causes duodenal ulcers and colitis and headaches; it is the way we respond to heavy traffic and telephones.

Sabre-toothed tigers can kill you with their claws or teeth. Gas bills can kill you only by the effect they have on your mind.

Each month something like six thousand medical journals are published around the world. And today a growing number of them are carrying reports of new evidence to illustrate the existence and importance of the vital link between mental pressure and physical and mental disease.

As far back as 1946 a research project started at Johns Hopkins University School of Medicine in Baltimore, involving nearly 1,500 medical students, was designed to investigate the relationship between attitudes and illness. The research programme lasted for seventeen years and suggested that the way an individual responds to pressure has a powerful effect on the types of illnesses his or her body develops.

Since then an overwhelming amount of evidence has been produced to show the truth of that assertion. At a conference hosted by the Department of Epidemiology and Rheumatology at McMaster University in Ontario, Canada, there was near unanimous agreement that a patient's attitudes towards life directly affect both his physical and mental health. It has even been shown that when people fall ill their worries about their illness are likely to produce yet further problems and delay the rate at which they get better. The link between the mind and the body can produce a constricting, destructive circle of endless physical and mental distress.

This relationship between the mind and the body is so close that, even when a disease or an injury seem to have been caused by some entirely external force, the attitude of the individual concerned can have a powerful effect on the speed with which the damaged parts of the body recover. If you fall down and break your leg, the rate at which your broken bones mend will depend upon your attitude, hopes, fears and aspirations. (In fact, they can also have an effect on whether or not you break your leg at all – but I'll come back to that later.)

A medical colleague of mine who works as a medical officer for a football club recently told me about two players in the team he looks after who had suffered very similar injuries after being tackled by rather ruthless opponents. The first player, Michael, was bitter and resentful and he was extremely angry because the opponent who had fouled him had been neither booked by the referee nor punished by his own club. He was worried too about his place in the side for which he normally played. He was well aware that a younger player in the reserves had taken full advantage of his opportunity to shine in the first team. He was aware that even when he had fully recovered he would still have to fight very hard to have a chance of regaining his place.

The second player, Tony, was much calmer about his injury. He accepted it as an occupational hazard and had plenty of confidence in his own ability to win back his place in the team. He spent hardly any time brooding about his injury, but concentrated instead on watching videotaped football games. He wanted desperately to play for his country and regarded the injury as nothing more than a temporary setback.

Within a couple of months Tony was back in the first team, fully recovered and hungry for success. Michael, the man who had spent his time sulking and worrying, was still walking with the aid of a stick. He looked like having a long, hard period of convalescence. There was a real risk that he would never play professional football again.

The power of the mind over the body can be so completely powerful that it can even affect an individual's will to live and his chances of staying alive. Most of us in the Western world think of voodoo as something of a joke. We think it slightly bizarre that there are still people living in Africa who can be so terrified by a threat uttered by a witch doctor that they will drop down dead within hours of being told that they will die.

And yet we are no different. It is just that our witch doctors, instead of wearing war paint, grass skirts and hideous masks, tend to wear dark trousers and white coats and have stethoscopes hanging round their necks. When a doctor tells us that we have three months to live or six months to live, or whatever, then the chances are that we will duly die on time.

Consider the true story of Lionel, for example. For several weeks Lionel had had a number of persistent and uncomfortable chest symptoms. He had a cough that wouldn't go away and he had some difficulty in getting his breath too. He had never had trouble with his chest before, but the symptoms seemed quite serious. Lionel's general practitioner tried all the usual antibiotics, but none of them seemed to make very much difference. Although he still managed to get to work, Lionel found his symptoms annoying, troublesome and tiring.

Fed up eventually with the persistent coughing and spluttering and weariness, Lionel asked his doctor to refer him to a specialist at the nearest hospital. He thought that perhaps a second opinion would provide him with a more permanent solution. He felt sure that someone, somewhere, ought to be able to tell him what was wrong – and then do something about it.

At the hospital the consultant looking after Lionel was puzzled, but recognizing that the symptoms were undoubtedly extremely troublesome he suggested that a few days in hospital might produce a proper diagnosis. Some sophisticated tests and X-rays might, he suggested, enable them to offer a satisfactory solution to the problem. Lionel readily accepted the consultant's offer, went into hospital and had a host of tests done.

After a week he was discharged and sent home. He was still no better than he had been when he had been admitted to the hospital, but at least he was no worse. And he was told that after he had been at home for a few days someone from the hospital would ring with the results of the tests.

It was five days after he'd gone back home before someone did ring. And the news was devastating. The hospital spokesman explained to Lionel's wife that the investigations had shown the presence of a fast-growing cancer for which no useful treatment could be offered. The hospital consultant had predicted a rapid decline and a death within a month or two at the outside.

This sad, frightening, unexpected and depressing news staggered Lionel and his family. They had not realized that the problem was so serious. Within two days of receiving the news

Lionel started to deteriorate. For the first time since the illness had begun he could not get out of bed. Work became impossible and he felt so weak that he could not eat properly. He began to lose weight so quickly that his family felt that he would be lucky to last out the week. He needed nursing night and day and complained of pains in his chest, arms and head. The family doctor offered pain killers, nursing aids and much-needed professional sympathy. Relatives came from distant parts of the country to await the predicted outcome.

And then came the second telephone call from the hospital. An apologetic voice told Lionel's wife that a mistake had been made and that Lionel didn't have cancer at all. Instead he had a rather rare type of chest infection – one that could be treated successfully with drugs. There had, explained the embarrassed hospital voice, been a mix-up between two sets of medical records belonging to patients with rather similar names.

Within twenty-four hours Lionel was out of bed and back at work. His appetite had come back, his pains had gone and he could walk perfectly easily. His weakness had entirely disappeared and he had been left with nothing more than the symptoms he'd started with: the cough and the breathlessness.

This dramatic but true story is by no means unusual. Daphne, for example, was told when she was small that she would always walk with a limp because she had one leg slightly shorter than the other. So she limped. Then at the age of twenty she visited a doctor who doubted the diagnosis. He had some fresh X-rays taken and was able to tell her that there was really nothing wrong with her legs. They were, according to the radiological evidence, exactly the same length. There were no abnormalities. When given this news Daphne lost the limp that she'd had for the best part of twenty years. Almost overnight she started to walk normally.

The writer T. H. White tells a story about an old man who lay on his death bed for days and days, only just alive but apparently unable to drift into the peace of death. Eventually, the old man's relatives remembered that around his neck the old man always wore a good luck charm. Throughout his life the man had never removed this charm, always believing that it gave him superhuman powers and provided him with some protection against death. When the chain was cut and the charm gently removed from around the old man's neck he died quickly and peacefully.

Earlier in this book I described how one of my patients had refused to die until satisfied that her children would be well looked after. But she wasn't the only patient I've looked after who defied death for her own personal, loving reasons.

Helen was separated from her husband and in her early forties when she developed cancer. It was a particularly virulent type of cancer and within months it had spread throughout her body. Every specialist she saw predicted that she would last no more than a matter of weeks. Every organ in her body was damaged, diseased and malfunctioning. The laboratory consultant at the nearby hospital found it quite remarkable that she was still alive at all, so severe was the damage that had been done.

And yet, despite the predictions of all the experts, Helen did not die. She had two small children to look after and she lived on. She repeatedly insisted that she would not and could not possibly die and leave them alone in the world. She would, she insisted, live and look after them. She looked terrible. The cancer ate away her body until there seemed to be more of the cancer than there was of her. And yet still she refused to die. In the end she survived until her children had both reached their teens and were old enough to go away to boarding school. And then she died. The post-mortem showed that there had been no mistake in the diagnosis. Every part of her body had been attacked by the cancer. She should have died years earlier.

Since it became clear that the mind does have power over the body, scientists have worked hard to try and show precisely how the functioning of the body can be influenced by transient thought processes. They have shown that it is through the medium of the imagination that the mind exerts much of its power. Our bodies are affected by what we think has happened, is happening or is likely to happen.

If you believe that you are going to be fired from your job, then your body will respond in as dramatic a way as if you are fired from your job. If you believe that you are pregnant, then your periods will stop, your breasts will swell and you will put on weight. Even if you do not have a developing foetus inside you.

Hypnotherapists have for years exploited the power of the

human imagination. A year or two ago I saw a stage hypnotherapist illustrate the power of the imagination very vividly. After calling for a volunteer from the audience, the hypnotherapist (or hypnotist I suppose he should really be called) told his volunteer to stand in the middle of the stage. He then talked quietly to him for a few seconds, perhaps a minute or so, and told the volunteer that he was relaxed, comfortable and ready to listen to suggestions.

The first trick that the hypnotist performed was really enough to convince me of the value of the skill he was exhibiting. He simply told the volunteer that his arms were too heavy to lift above his head. I happened to know the volunteer and I rather suspected that he would be difficult to hypnotize. I certainly knew that he would not agree to do anything just to make the hypnotist look good. But, to my amazement, when he tried to lift his arms above his head he couldn't. They really did look as if they were too heavy to be moved.

Since then I've seen many other examples of the way that hypnotism and hypnotherapy can work. I've hypnotized people myself. And there is absolutely no doubt that it is a potent force. I have seen a volunteer convinced, under hypnosis, that a piece of ice is a red-hot poker. And I've seen that volunteer develop a blister and burn when touched by the piece of ice. The body reacts to the suggestion and not to the reality.

Hypnotherapy is often associated with Svengali-like figures, darkened rooms with drawn curtains, soft voices, swinging fob watches and long leather couches. It is often associated with charlatans, quacks, cheap diplomas, quick profits and dishonest practitioners. But it is, in fact, a genuine way of using the power of the imagination.

The first evidence to show that hypnotherapy can have useful effects was produced in 1847, when James Esdale performed 300 major surgical operations in India using no anaesthetic other than hypnosis. Since then, evidence has accumulated all around the world to show that by hypnotizing patients and putting them into an altered state of conscious-ness it is possible to combat many different kinds of pain and discomfort.

Scientists have also performed experiments proving that the power of the imagination is so complete that apparently involuntary reflexes can be controlled by thought processes. For example, it seems that the body's digestive processes can be controlled by imagination. In one experiment which was conducted a year or two ago volunteers were able to produce enzymes which their bodies did not need. Normally, if human beings eat meals that contain a good deal of fat, their bodies produce special enzymes which break down the fat and turn it into products which can be readily transported in the blood. Those enzymes are produced without any thought; their production is controlled by a sophisticated series of reflexes. Under experimental conditions, however, it was shown that if volunteers were told that they had eaten fat when they hadn't, their bodies would respond to the imagined truth rather than the real truth. The fat-dissolving enzymes were produced.

In another experiment it was shown that the body's immune system can be controlled by using the imagination too. Normally when human beings are given an intradermal tuberculin injection to find out whether or not they are immune to T.B., their bodies respond automatically. If the individual has been previously exposed to tuberculosis and has prepared internal immune defence systems, a swelling and a small red mark will develop at the site. If the individual has not previously been exposed to T.B. and has not developed any immune defences, no mark and no swelling will develop. This test is done routinely to find out whether patients need vaccinations to help provide them with protection against T.B.

And yet researchers have shown that the body's apparently entirely involuntary response to the testing injection can be regulated by the imagination. If an individual who would normally have reacted to an intradermal injection of tuber-culin is told not to respond, his body does not respond. The swelling and the red mark do not develop. The imagination can, it seems, even control a cell-mediated immunity reaction.

In my medical practice I've seen plenty of clinical evidence of the way that the immune system can be influenced by the imagination. A patient of mine called Malcolm was a constant sufferer from hay fever. He was allergic to a huge number of different types of plant but his main problem seemed to be flowers. Whenever he got close to flowers of any kind, he would sneeze and sneeze and sneeze. His eyes would run and he would look and sound extremely uncomfortable. His allergy got so bad that he only had to see a bunch of flowers to start sneezing.

Hay fever is, of course, an allergy disorder that depends to a large extent upon the body's immune defence systems getting out of control. The body for some reason recognizes pollen as an enemy and prepares its own defences. The idea is to get rid of the pollen as quickly as possible and the symptoms of hay fever are designed to do just that. Tears are produced to wash pollen away from the eyes and sneezes are started to empty the nose. It is an efficient overreaction.

Theoretically, of course, these responses will not start unless the pollen is present. But I managed to prove that Malcolm's problems weren't purely physical when he came into the surgery one day and started sneezing because of a vase full of flowers that a patient had left in the reception area. The flowers were artificial. Malcolm's imagination had done the rest.

Since there is now a growing amount of evidence to suggest that the body's immune system may well be linked to the development of many of the most destructive diseases of the twentieth century – including rheumatoid arthritis and some forms of cancer – the significance of this link between the imagination and the body's immune responses cannot be overestimated.

If the imagination can have such a powerful effect, its strength as a healing power must surely match its damaging potential. The most remarkable thing about the imagination is perhaps the way that we have been aware of its power without really recognizing the importance of that power. It really isn't difficult to think of plenty of other examples of ways in which the imagination rules the body.

If you put a wooden plank on the floor and try to walk along it, you'll find it a remarkably easy task. Now, try telling yourself that the plank is suspended fifty feet above the floor. And that there are wild tigers waiting underneath for you to fall. The plank won't have altered in width or height above the floor. But you'll find walking along it a much more difficult and daunting task.

Football managers also know the value of the human imagination. If a player's mind tells him that he is tired, he will be tired. And he will find it difficult to keep running in the second half of the game. If all the players in a team believe that they are going to lose they will probably lose. If all the players in a team believe that they are going to win, they will probably win. The half-time pep talk can make a staggering amount of difference to a team's success. The team manager or captain who can instil a sense of confidence and quiet determination in his team will be well worth his place for his qualities of leadership alone.

Film directors have for years exploited the power of the human imagination without really being fully aware of the strength of the power they have at their disposal. When a cinema patron settles down in his seat to enjoy a good film, he will be lost in the fantasy world that has been created for him. As long as the film is a good one, and is convincing, each member of the audience will forget that he is sitting in a darkened room with several hundred other people. He won't hear the rustling of toffee papers or the crackle of popcorn. The illusion created on the screen will be enough to enable him to escape from the real world in which his body is imprisoned. His mind will wander freely, directed by the actions of the figures on the screen. And what is happening in his mind will rule what happens to his body too.

When the film *Lawrence of Arabia* was shown on the cinema screen, reports from around the world indicated that the sale of ice-cream in those cinemas had rocketed. The endless desert scenes had made the patrons feel uncomfortably hot. Their bodies had responded to what they thought they were seeing and experiencing, and during the intervals thousands of people had bought themselves cooling ice-creams.

You can see this influence for yourself next time there is a film on the television at home. If, for example, the film shows shots of icy wastes and explorers huddled together in tents, you'll probably see the people with you shivering, moaning about the cold and switching on the fire. If the film is frightening with shots of dark passageways, hidden terrors, vampires, murderers and other threats, the people with you will be biting their finger nails, covering their eyes with their hands and rushing out during the advertisements to check that the back door is firmly locked and bolted.

And you can obtain the same sort of genuine physical

response by reading a good book. If the story is frightening, you'll feel your pulse racing and the hairs standing up on the back of your neck and the backs of your hands. If the story is sad, the tears will start to pour down your cheeks. Your body will have responded to your imagination.

For some years now scientists in a number of very reputable institutes around the world have been producing evidence to show that patients who meditate and relax are often capable of dealing with the sort of disorders known to be associated with stress and pressure. Under laboratory conditions there is absolutely no doubt that people who relax themselves thoroughly can reduce their blood pressure, slow down their heart rate and generally increase their ability to cope with pressure without becoming ill.

From the research evidence available it seems that modern life is so fast and so frenetic, so totally unforgiving, that most of us push ourselves too far and too quickly. We do not allow ourselves time to accustom ourselves to our lifestyles; we do not allow ourselves time to unwind; and we do not allow ourselves the chance to soothe our minds (and therefore our bodies) with gentle, pleasing, relaxing images.

There are, I think, three main reasons why the advantages of thorough relaxation have not been enjoyed by a wider audience. First, the word 'relaxation' tends to cause a good deal of confusion and misunderstanding. Many people assume that if they sit down in front of the television set with a sandwich and a beer, they are relaxing.

In fact, of course, that sort of relaxation may well help the body – but it doesn't help the mind very much. And as I have already shown, it is the mind that rules the body. Lying down in a stupor in front of the television won't do very much to soothe the troubled mind. The images of the day's problems will continue to fight for space alongside the images being projected by the evening's television programmes. The television news will be full of terrible new worries to be added to the ones already clamouring for attention. It is hardly surprising that after an evening in front of the television set many people need sleeping pills to help them get to sleep at night. I do wish that the television companies would bring back the old-fashioned 'interlude'. It would, I feel quite sure, make a tremendous difference to the quality of life for most viewers. Played once an hour for five minutes the interlude would give viewers a chance to rest their minds very effectively.

Second, the religious and semi-religious features which seem to be an essential part of many forms of meditation are frightening and forbidding to many people. The words 'relaxation' and 'meditation' have become linked with shaven-headed mystics, religious groups and orange-robed eccentrics. It is hardly surprising that many people shy away from either concept. They want to know how to deal with life. They don't want to take part in any organized rituals and they would feel self-conscious if they had to sing or chant any magic incantations.

Many who try to introduce meditation into our culture make the simple mistake of trying to introduce a technique devised for an Eastern culture. Repetitive dance and chant rhythms have been used by primitive tribes around the world for centuries (and have been used very effectively too, with a loss of self-awareness and an accompanying sense of soothing relaxation), but they were never suitable for mass marketing in the Western world.

Third, those who have talked about the values of meditation have constantly claimed that it is necessary to empty the mind of all inputs and all thoughts in order to benefit from the respite. And that is not easy. Many people find the prospect of emptying their minds so daunting that they never even try.

These three drawbacks have resulted in meditation and relaxation remaining the prerogative of a relatively small number of individuals. And that is a terrible shame, for millions could undoubtedly benefit from using techniques of this type. Meditation helps by triggering off the body's own quite natural relaxation response – the natural antithesis to the stress response. And it is ironic that although most of us put our bodies and our minds under more pressure than our ancestors ever had to face we have forgotten how to use these natural techniques for opposing pressure.

Another factor that has a powerful influence on the way that an individual responds to stressful situations is the nature of his or her personality. Indeed, not only is there now plenty of evidence to show that the personality of an individual can have a tremendous influence on the way that his or her body responds to stress, pressure and environmental problems, but there is also evidence to show that the personality of an individual can have an effect on the type of illness he subsequently develops.

Some of the research evidence linking personality type to specific types of disease is very old. In 1910 William Osler wrote in *The Lancet* that it was ambitious, hard-working men who were most likely to develop heart trouble. And in 1945 it was suggested that people who have heart attacks are often tortured by their need to compete with their fathers.

Since then a growing number of researchers have managed to amplify both these statements. In her book *Biotypes* (London, 1981), for example, Joan Arehart-Treichel tells how in the early 1950s an unholsterer repairing chairs in a reception room shared by two doctors noticed that only the front edges of the chairs were worn – as though the patients who had been sitting there had all been literally 'on edge'. The two doctors were called Rosenman and Friedman and they spent a large part of the next two decades trying to find out more about the type of patients likely to have heart attacks.

They discovered that the people who were getting heart attacks were usually male and commonly under great pressure. They also managed to show that these men invariably had a strong drive to compete and to achieve. The heart attack patient, it seems, works long hours, sets out to succeed, finds it difficult to sit still, is unable to relax and is a perfectionist. No matter how successful he is, he will rarely be able to satisfy his ambitions. And, of course, it's not how successful you are that determines your sense of personal satisfaction - it is how successful you think you are.

The evidence linking personality to cancer also goes back a long way. In the second century AD the Roman physician Galen noticed that women who were depressed were far more likely to develop cancer than women who were happy. In recent years we've acquired considerable evidence to support that early observation. Today it is known that the people who are cancer-prone tend to try too hard to please the world. When they fail, as they invariably must (simply because it is never possible to please everybody all the time), they are more likely to develop cancer.

Cancer sufferers often have unhappy childhoods and frequently grow up suffering from a lack of love, a sense of loneliness and a feeling that they have been deserted by those closest to them. Cancer victims tend to give more than they take; they tend to repress their own desires and their own emotional feelings. Unselfishly, they do their best to please those around them and when anything goes wrong with the world they have created, they develop cancer.

There is evidence showing that it is possible to link specific personality types to all sorts of diseases – arthritis, asthma, colitis, eczema, hay fever and migraine, for example. And there is even evidence to show that there are personality factors which determine who is most likely to suffer from colds and minor throat and chest infections. Dr Richard Totman of Sussex University and Dr Donald Broadbent of Oxford, working with the Common Cold Research Unit in England, have come to the conclusion that introverts are far more likely to get lots of colds than extroverts, and that people who are obsessional are particularly likely to get colds. It seems that the severity of the symptoms endured by someone who has a cold depends upon the amount of stress and strain he thinks he is under.

Not only are specific types of personality linked to specific physical conditions but there is also a great deal of evidence showing that the personality of an individual will have an influence on the lifestyle he follows, the type of partner he chooses and the sort of work he selects for himself.

The individual's personality may help ensure that his life follows a certain, fairly well-defined pattern. But at the same time it may mean that he comes face to face with a regular series of stresses and problems.

Take Henry, for example. At the age of sixteen he knew he wanted to spend his life working with figures. He loved mathematics at school and obtained a considerable amount of satisfaction from fairly tedious, routine work with figures. By the time he was twenty-five he was well established in an office with a firm of accountants. It was the sort of work he had always wanted to do. And, in a way, it was the sort of work that he was cut out to do best.

Yet by the time Henry came to see me his work had done a

considerable amount of damage to his health. He had a nasty inflammatory disease of the large bowel called colitis – a disease commonly associated with stress and pressure. Henry's problem was that although he enjoyed his work, he also took it very seriously. He got very upset when errors crept into the columns of figures in front of him. If at the end of a day's work he had one set of accounts that were a penny out he would lie awake at night worrying about it. His obsessional personality meant that he was perfectly well suited to the work he did. But his obsessional personality also meant that the work he did was making him ill.

And Henry was no no means an isolated case. During the years I spent in general practice I came across hundreds of patients whose lives had been mapped out for them by their personalities. And in many cases the lifestyles those patients had chosen for themselves had ended up crippling or destroying them.

Our personalities play a vitally important role in our lives. They determine the sort of immediate environment we create for ourselves and they then determine the way in which we respond to the stresses and strains that are inherent in that self-made environment. It is our minds which commonly kill our bodies. But it is our personalities which decide just how the killing is done.

In some ways the human memory is extraordinarily inefficient. But in many ways it is extremely efficient. Different people seem able to remember different things in entirely different ways – and with different degrees of success. Wine tasters store the memory of the taste of scores of wines. Art historians can store images quite clearly in their minds. Musicians retain scores and arrangements. Tailors can retain the 'feel' of certain types of cloth. Cooks and gourmets can remember certain types of smell.

And, of course, a person who has a particularly good memory in one respect may be devoid of it in another respect. I once had a patient who could remember every football match his favourite first division side had ever played. He could tell you the result of every league match and every cup match. He could tell you whether the match had been played at home or away from home. He could tell you the players on each side and the final and half-time scores. And he could remember matches and scorelines from years ago. In this respect his memory was faultless.

Yet he couldn't remember how to do simple tasks when he was at work. He couldn't even remember how to operate the machine he was supposed to be minding. After listening to him talk about football matches you'd have thought he was a genius. But after listening to his foreman describe his failings at work you'd have thought him more likely to be mentally deficient.

The reason why our memories change so much – and why my patient had such an efficient memory for football matches and such an appalling memory for work – is that our memories are often mixed up with emotions, feelings, attitudes and prejudices. Those emotions and attitudes influence the way we respond to specific incidents and they influence the way that those events stay in our minds. My patient remembered all his team's football matches because he was desperately interested in football in general and in the success of his side in particular. When he talked about a particular match he could 'see' it taking place. He could remember whether he was happy or sad at the time. But he had no interest at all in the work he was doing. And there were no emotional aids to help him remember what the foreman had told him. Memories are influenced in this way quite frequently and the result is that our attitudes towards new events and incidents and stresses can be controlled not simply by straightforward past memories, but by memories which have been distorted by association as well as by time.

I hardly ever wear a suit, but recently, as a joke, I put on a three-piece pin-stripe suit that I hadn't worn for years. A television producer with whom I was working had complained that I always turned up at the studios wearing a jumper and that I needed to look more like a doctor. I thought that the three-piece pin-striped suit, together with a blue-and-white spotted bow tie, might produce a smile or two.

As it happened, however, the suit was the one I wore when I attended my first medical school interview. And it was the one I'd worn for my medical school examinations. I'd hardly ever worn it except for interviews and other equally important engagements. Physically the suit still fitted fairly comfortably.

But, nevertheless, I felt distinctly uncomfortable as soon as I put it on. Theoretically, it wasn't any different from just wearing a sports jacket, waistcoat and trousers. But to me it brought back fears, anxieties, long-forgotten worries. Past memories and associations flooded back. And I felt uncomfortable and rather nervous. My stomach started rumbling and my heart started beating faster than usual. I wasn't going anywhere threatening or doing anything worrying, but my body (under the influence of my mind) was responding as though I was going to an important interview.

If you stop and think about it for a minute or two, you'll realize that this sort of thing happens quite a lot. If you go out to buy some new furniture and the salesman reminds you of someone who always used to annoy you – perhaps he looks like a particularly obnoxious prefect at school, for example – then you'll be critical and suspicious and you probably won't buy furniture from him however hard he tries or however good a bargain he offers you.

If, however, you are served by a salesman who reminds you more of a close friend, you'll feel much warmer towards him, and you'll probably buy something even if you aren't offered a good price. Unless, that is, the salesman is unfortunate enough to trigger off some unhappy memory while he gives you his sales pitch. If, for example, he asks you about your holidays and you've just come back from a really miserable two weeks in Spain during which time you caught all sorts of nasty diseases, were mugged, found yourself staying in a half-finished hotel and didn't have an edible forkful of food, then you'll lose some of your good humour and unconsciously you'll begin to dislike him.

While writing this book, I spent a good deal of time touring around Devon and Cornwall looking for a new home and I noticed this phenomenon at work on numerous occasions. When I went into a house where the people were warm and friendly, I was favourable impressed by the house – even if it had woodworm, damp and dry rot. When I went into homes where the people were cold and unfriendly – or, more important, reminded me of people who had annoyed me or been unkind to me in the past – I was not very enthusiastic about their houses.

We will also respond to simple things like a smile or a scowl, simply because our minds (and our memories) tell us that a smile suggests that things are going to go smoothly, while a scowl suggests that things are going to go badly. This phenomenon is illustrated neatly by a true anecdote.

Inspired by research which shows that our behaviour can be influenced by the behaviour of other people, and by our interpretation of that behaviour as determined by our association between memories and circumstances, a group of American psychology students decided to play a trick on their psychology professor.

When he was lecturing, the professor habitually walked about the lecture theatre, usually wandering from one side to the other many times during a single one-hour lecture. So the students decided to start behaving differently according to the corner of the room that the professor was occupying. When he was in the left-hand corner of the lecture theatre, all the students smiled at him and listened attentively to what he had to say. When he was in the other corner, they were noisy and inattentive. Within a remarkably short space of time he was doing all his lecturing standing in just one spot. You won't need any help to guess which corner he chose.

The mind-controlling factors which I've discussed so far have been both explicable and understandable. But there are many aspects of the human mind that are far from explicable, for the human mind has skills, strengths and powers that we have as yet only glimpsed. For example, have you ever noticed that if you are at a party where dozens of people are talking loudly and someone mentions your name, your ears will automatically prick up? You will have isolated the sounds of your name from the general hubbub, even though you hadn't consciously been listening to the conversation concerned.

From research done in the last few years it seems that our hearing acuity is very much more powerful than any of us might have imagined. In one fascinating experiment, volunteers listened to various numbers being read out on a piece of recording tape. Every time the number five was mentioned a puff of air was blown on to the eyelids of the volunteers. Eventually, the individuals all acquired reflexes which meant that they blinked whenever they heard the number five on the tape.

That was straightforward enough. But the next part of the experiment was really remarkable. For the people who had organized the experiment discovered that when they turned down the tape recorder and played it so that the voice on it was inaudible, the volunteers still blinked every time the number five was mentioned. Somehow they had managed to hear unconsciously what they had been unable to detect consciously.

Since the remarkable Uri Geller startled the world with his metal-bending experiments numerous researchers around the world have done experiments with other individuals and produced similar results. At London University's Birkbeck College, for example, Professor John Hasted has tested over twenty youngsters, using sophisticated electronic sensors to prevent trickery and to filter out the effects of freak atmospheric conditions and electrical interference. He, and other scientists around the world, have confirmed that many individuals do have quite remarkable and totally inexplicable powers. Cameramen working with film crews recording such experiments have reported that their equipment has frequently been broken or distorted.

And countless scientists are now prepared to confirm that extra-sensory perception can no longer be dismissed as merely a piece of science fiction. There are many authenticated stories illustrating this aspect of the mind's unexplained power.

In Saratoga, California, a forty-nine-year-old widow, asleep in her flat, suddenly woke up at 2 a.m. after dreaming of a burning house full of elderly people running about in their nightwear. The dream was so realistic that she felt that she had to do something about it. Feeling rather foolish she dressed quickly and drove off to the first of three old peoples' homes that she helped to run, anxious to make sure that there was nothing wrong.

In a small room at the back of one of these houses she found flames shooting out of a gas main. No one could have possibly seen the fire, and the fire brigade chief who dealt with the blaze said that within half an hour the blaze would have destroyed the house, killing many of the inhabitants.

No one yet can explain this type of phenomenon, but nor do many scientists deny that these things take place. Indeed, although there are no certain answers available, some answers

71

and explanations do seem to be emerging. At the Maudsley Hospital in London, for example, Dr Peter Fenwick and his colleagues have found significant numbers of head injuries, episodes of being knocked unconscious, blackouts and serious illnesses in the medical histories of the mediums they have studied. From their work it seems that there is a link between an individual being knocked unconscious and that individual later showing skills at telepathy or clairvoyance.

Good scientists tend to greet all new ideas and partly substantiated theories with a healthy mixture of scepticism and fear. But I believe that there is now convincing evidence to support the theory that a sixth sense does exist and that such things as extra-sensory perception, telepathy and premonitions are as real as vision and hearing. The capacities of the sense organs we know about are far greater than we might have suspected a few years ago. The capacities of the sense organs we have not yet identified are so vast that it is unwise at this stage even to attempt to define any boundaries.

The strength of the evidence in existence can no longer be ignored. Human beings have the capacity to transmit and receive messages through their minds and they have the capacity to affect matter through the power of their minds alone. These truths may sit uncomfortably beside traditional scientific teachings, and we may not understand how these mechanisms operate. But their existence can no longer be denied.

So far most of the practical evidence I've produced has illustrated the destructive effect that the mind can have on the body. But there is also a staggering amount of evidence to show that the power of the mind can have a remarkably constructive, healing effect on the body too. The powers that can stimulate the development of disease can be used to stimulate the body's self-healing processes and to protect an individual from all sorts of diseases and disorders. The very same powers that can produce devastating damage can also be used to prevent illness developing and to deal with problems which have already started.

When I was a medical student I remember a physiology lecturer who used to push a metal spike into his biceps to show us the electrical effects produced by a muscle contracting. He used to do this as a regular part of his teaching course and he never bled nor seemed to suffer any pain. The spike was about as long as a knitting needle and the lecturer would push it right into his arm without so much as a flinch or a moment's hesitation.

I was impressed by that memory for many years, but never really understood how the lecturer had done it. And then, quite recently, I came across another physician, this time an American, who had had a similar experience while still a medical student. His lecturer had also pushed a metal skewer about the length of a knitting needle straight through the centre of his biceps muscle without losing so much as a drop of blood and without suffering in any obvious way at all.

This student, more courageous and perhaps more curious than I had been at the time, had asked his lecturer to explain just how he had managed to perform such an extraordinary feat.

The lecturer had duly explained that every time he performed the experiment he would mentally place himself in a far corner of the room so that he wouldn't feel any pain as the spike went through his muscle. And he would leave behind instructions that his body's defences would deal with any infection introduced into the muscle and also ensure that any blood vessels damaged by the spike entering the skin would be closed up immediately without blood loss.

This wasn't a crazy circus performer talking. It was an ordinary physiology lecturer talking to a medical school student. And although only an anecdote, it does, I think, illustrate the extent to which the mind can influence the body's susceptibility to infection and disease. Both those lecturers were, of course, way ahead of their time. A year or two ago the majority of medical academics would have still found it difficult to believe that the mind could have such control over the body.

But in the last year or two a number of scientific papers have been published showing that the mind does have this quite remarkable power over what happens to the body. For example, the imagination can exert a deep and lasting influence over the body's ability to acquire simple physical skills.

In an experiment conducted in Australia in 1983,

73

researchers took a large group of people who had absolutely nothing in common apart from the fact that none of them had ever played basketball before. After being allowed to spend one day throwing basketballs through a hoop the volunteers were divided into three separate groups. The first group were told to play absolutely no basketball for a month. They were told not even to think about basketball. The second group were told to practise every day. And the third group were told to spend ten minutes a day imagining that they were throwing balls into a basket.

At the end of the one-month experiment the people in the first group were no better at basketball than they had been at the start of the whole exercise. However, the other two groups had improved by closely similar amounts. The players who had been spending their time out on the court throwing basketballs through hoops had improved by 24 per cent. And the players who had spent ten minutes a day imagining that they had been throwing basketballs through hoops had improved by 23 per cent.

Even more impressive has been the work done in America by Dr Carl Simonton and his wife. For a number of years now they have been teaching patients how to cope with cancer by using their imaginations. The theory is that if the imagination can have a destructive effect, it can also have a positive effect. If people can give themselves cancer by negative thinking, they should be able to protect themselves against cancer and maybe even cure themselves of cancer by positive thinking. If people can give themselves cancer by being miserable and sad, perhaps they can help get themselves better by being happy and cheerful. In the first years of their experiment the Simontons have found that their patients have lived, on average, more than a year longer than patients who were not encouraged to use their minds to help fight their disease.

All around the world research is beginning to come up with similarly impressive results. Growing numbers of doctors and healers of all kinds are finding that the mind can protect the body, help it to fight off ill health and help it to conquer and defeat disease.

At the start of this book I explained how I had first been made aware of the way in which the human mind can regulate the body's responses. Because just about every single physical disorder that affects us is influenced in one way or another by the mind, the influences of these mental powers are far-reaching and exhaustive. Mindpower is, I believe, a positive force which can help any patient under any circumstances. No longer do we have to be spectators at our illnesses.

I hope that by now I will have convinced you that your mind has power over your body. And I hope that you understand that if you learn how to use your mental powers to the full, you will become both physically and mentally stronger; you will be happier, healthier and far less vulnerable to disease than you would otherwise have been. Mindpower is a marriage between traditional philosophies and modern technologies and it offers a safe, genuine solution to the special rigours and threats of twentieth-century life.

At its simplest level mindpower can help you deal with many of the common physical troubles which seem to plague us all. If you know that your indigestion is caused by worry, it is obviously more logical to do something about your worry (or the way that you respond to the things which are worrying you) than it is simply to keep on treating the indigestion. The old-fashioned, interventionist, approach was to pour bottles of antacid into an acid-filled stomach to quell the symptoms. That was, I believe, about as logical as repapering the bedroom ceiling because of problems caused by a leaky roof.

The link between the mind and the body is so complex that you don't have to be under stress to develop stress-induced symptoms of distress – you need only to imagine that you are under stress. You don't have to be unemployed to develop physical symptoms. You need only worry about being made redundant. You don't need to be penniless. You need only worry that you might become penniless. You don't need to feel tense to develop a headache. You need only worry that you will become tense. You don't need to be pregnant to miss a period. You need only worry that you might be pregnant. Once you genuinely believe that you have problems, your body will respond as though the problems were real. You will develop physical symptoms of a real illness. An entirely imaginary problem can cause potentially lethal, physical changes to take place.

And so the strength of mindpower can operate at a far more

sophisticated level. You can become genuinely ill by worrying and by imagining that dreadful things are going to happen. But you can also keep yourself fit and help yourself get better when you are ill by using the power of your imagination to help you support your body's self-healing mechanisms.

This capacity of the imagination to help us fight illness is still something that we do not fully understand. And it is something that many still find difficult to accept. Most people readily understand that the mind can have a destructive effect on the body. But fewer are prepared to acknowledge that the mind can have an equally powerful constructive effect.

If you still remain sceptical, stop for a while and read through some of the preceding pages again. Try to remember that one of the problems we all face when trying to come to terms with the power of the mind is that these new theories and principles of life defy just about everything we were taught when we were small. And yet to ignore these truths simply because they do not fit in with what we used to regard as the truth is foolish.

During the last half a century we have all learned to accept a growing number of things which we can neither explain nor understand. We accept that television programmes are transmitted around the world although most of us do not understand how it happens. We accept that men walk on the moon. Although we don't know just how it is done. We accept that aeroplanes fly faster than the speed of sound. We accept that radios can pick up signals through house walls. We accept the telephone and the electric light bulb. So why should we remain sceptical about the unseen powers of our minds? Why should we stay blind to the irony that although our minds can make us ill our minds can make us better?

In recent years exercising the body has become something of a religion. Thousands of people exercise their bodies regularly in attempts to become fit and to avoid ill health. But I believe that you can do far more for your health by learning to exercise your mind and use it properly and effectively than you can by exercising your body. Far more disorders are caused by mental pressures than are caused by a lack of physical exercise. By using your natural mindpower you can deal with those pressures and maintain good health. You can learn how to treat the vast majority of problems likely to affect your body without asking for help from any sort of interventionist. And you can improve your chances of survival when you do need to seek outside help.

Mindpower is an effective source of primary health care. Learn to harness the hidden healing powers of your mind and you can learn to control your health.

CHAPTER 5

Using your mind to heal your body – controlling negative forces

Sadness

One common emotional response to pressure and stress is sorrow. Sadness is our way of reacting to problems which affect us in a deeply personal way. The natural, human way of responding to sadness is by crying. When we are small and unhappy, we cry naturally to make it clear to those who are close to us and near to us that we need sympathy and attention. Gradually, as we grow older we find that by shedding tears we gain sympathy, love and affection: all the things which help us live with and overcome our sadness.

Not that tears simply provide an emotional release. They also provide a genuine, physical release. According to a number of researchers who specialize in the subject of grief, and who attended a recent meeting of the American Psychological Association in Washington, emotionally shed tears don't just provide an important stress relief valve – they also help the body get rid of harmful chemical wastes.

In studies done with both men and women Dr William H. Frey of the St Paul-Ramsey Medical Centre found that tears that were shed for emotional reasons have a higher protein content than tears shed because of winds, specks of dust and other sources of irritation. It is clear, therefore, that crying is a useful and constructive way of dealing with sadness.

However, because crying is such an obvious physical sign of distress many people regard it as a sign of weakness and emotional instability. Boys are often taught that it is un-forgivable to cry in public and that they should bottle up their feelings rather than let themselves be seen with tears on their cheeks. Politicians have ruined their careers by shedding a tear or two at an inappropriate moment. Sadly, but perhaps predictably, the evidence also shows that when children or adults do not cry they suffer badly when under pressure. People who don't cry because they consider it unacceptable end up not only suppressing their tears but also their emotions.

The damage is done in three ways: first, the storing up of tears means that unwanted chemical wastes are not excreted; second, the failure to cry means that much-needed love and attention is not obtained; and third the sense of emotional release through crying is also missed. Most people will confirm that after crying they feel calm, rested in a strange sort of way, and much happier about their original problems, fears and worries.

The conclusion from all the available evidence has to be that crying is an excellent way of dealing with sadness and sorrow. Individuals who suppress their natural instinct to cry are increasing their chances of acquiring a stress-related disorder. If you have acquired the habit of suppressing tears when you feel them welling up inside you, try to get out of the habit; try to let yourself go next time you feel upset. Crying is nothing to be ashamed of. And if you are close to someone who never cries, try to persuade him that crying is neither unnatural nor unmanly.

Anger

Anger is a common response to anything which produces physical or mental pain. It is one of the commonest, most fundamental human feelings. It can be produced by our own shortcomings, by disappointments, by frustrations and by what we see as injustices. It is inspired by aggressive ticket collectors, surly car park attendants, officious police officers, rude, indifferent bureaucrats, mean-minded clerks, impatient drivers, thoughtless relatives and unreasonable employers.

Whatever causes it, anger is often physically, mentally, socially and economically damaging. An angry man will raise his voice and become irascible; his face will become red, he will fidget and move around more than usual and, since fear commonly accompanies anger, he will sweat too. Stored, unexpressed anger produces high blood pressure and all the other symptoms of stress-induced disease. The extra flow of acid into the stomach may help produce an ulcer and persistent anger can produce mental symptoms such as insomnia. Anger is so often linked to pain and discomfort that it is no coincidence that we turn the relationship round and describe red, painful burns and wounds as looking 'angry'.

Many diseases are produced by anger. High blood pressure, heart attacks and strokes are all common consequences of uncontrolled anger. The eighteenth-century surgeon John Hunter correctly predicted that his life was at the mercy of anyone who 'put him in a passion'. He died at a meeting of hospital administrators.

Today we know that anger doesn't only produce disease in this direct and straightforward way. There is now plenty of evidence around to show that any individual who suppresses his anger will be more likely to develop cancer than an individual who responds to his anger in a more natural and emotional way. Among the many studies done, one at the Institute of Psychiatry in London has shown that women who suppress their anger are more prone to develop breast cancer than women who let their feelings out when they are angry or upset.

Anger is a killer. And in order to reduce its damaging effects it is vitally important to know just how to deal with it safely and effectively. There are four things to remember if you want to learn how to control the negative force of anger.

1   Accept the fact that you, like everyone else, will get angry from time to time. Anger is a perfectly natural and reasonably healthy response to stressful circumstances. It is no sin to get angry – although it may be a sin to allow your anger to take over your emotions completely Remember that it is dangerous to suppress your anger and to refuse to acknowledge its existence.

2   Learn to recognize when you are heading towards a confrontation and, if possible, avoid stressful situations. Don't push other people into a position where they cannot easily escape without a tremendous loss of face. Decide as early as possible whether or not the subject is worth getting excited about. If you pick your problems carefully, your anger will be

justifiable and possibly effective and you will suffer far less.

3 If you feel angry and you believe that your anger is justified, don't suppress it all – let it out.

Dr Sheldon Tobin, Associate Professor at the School of Social Service Administration at the University of Chicago, found that the nursing home patients most likely to survive are those patients who are most aggressive, irritating and demanding. The passive, gentle individuals who never complain and who always accept everything that happens to them tend to die sooner.

If your doctor tells you something you don't like, make it clear that you don't like what he's told you. If he tells you that you've got three months to live, make it damned clear that you object to his arrogance. Let your anger out and make up your mind to show him whether he can tell you know long you've got to live! (Paradoxically, getting angry with your doctor will often cement your relationship with him. And if it ruins the relationship, it doesn't really matter does it? If he doesn't understand how you feel and doesn't respond to your reactions, his presence is hardly helping you.)

Some experts have, in the past, argued that it is sensible to count to ten before acting or speaking when feeling angry. It would now seem that this is a rather counter-productive technique. It doesn't stop anger producing damaging effects, but merely hides the consequences and, in the end, leads to greater problems. The best response to anger is neither to hide it nor to allow it to turn into an uncontrolled explosion of noise and unhappiness, but to get rid of it by making specific, powerful complaints and expressing your anger and frustration in as positive a manner as possible.

Don't be a wimp, but don't be a boar either!

4 If you feel anger building up inside you and you feel tempted to get rid of it in some physical way, follow your natural instincts as far as possible. I don't suggest that you race round and hit whoever it is who has annoyed you. But you can get rid of your excess energy and anger by taking part in some hectic and energetic sporting activity. Hitting a squash or tennis ball or kicking a football can all be pretty good ways to get rid of aggressive feelings. Or you can paint the face of someone you dislike on to a punchball – and then try hitting the stuffing out of them.

Alternatively, try chopping up some firewood in the garden. Or hanging out a few carpets and giving them a good beating. Or digging over a patch of garden. Or taking a pile of old plates into the garage or down the garden and smashing them one by one. Whichever technique you choose, getting rid of aggressive feelings will leave you far healthier than if you allow your feelings to build up inside you.

Symptoms of ill health

When I first started as a general practitioner some fifteen years ago one of the first patients I saw was a six-year-old boy called William who was suffering from intermittent abdominal pains. According to his mother, the pains never lasted for more than a few hours but they were always fairly severe. I examined William but could find absolutely nothing wrong with him, so I asked his mother to telephone me the next time the pains developed.

She rang me the following Sunday evening, at about nine o'clock, to tell me that her son was in bed and in considerable pain. Suspecting a possible appendicitis, I leaped into my motor car and drove round to their house just as quickly as I was able. After a thorough examination I had to confess that I still couldn't find anything wrong. But William's pains were so severe that I thought he ought to be in hospital so I made all the necessary arrangements.

On the following Monday morning, after my surgery was finished, I called in at the hospital to see how my young patient was. I half expected to find that the surgeons had removed his appendix. To my surprise, however, William wasn't even in the hospital. The consultant surgeon had sent him back home again.

'He'd had these pains several times before,' explained the surgeon, 'and they'd always developed on a Sunday evening. I thought it was rather odd, so I asked his mother how long the pains usually lasted. She said that they invariably lasted until about mid-way through Monday morning.'

And that, the surgeon explained, had given him the clue.

'Every fourth Monday our young friend and all his chums have a spelling test,' the surgeon continued. 'Like most of us, he doesn't particularly like examinations . . .'

Slowly, the truth dawned on me.

Young William had been 'using' his abdominal pains as an excuse for not having to put up with his monthly spelling test. He wasn't playing ill deliberately, but his mind had learned that if he showed signs of abdominal pain, he would not only gain a good deal of extra sympathy and love from his mother, but he would also be allowed to stay at home and avoid his examination.

'So, what do we do?' his mother and father wanted to know when I saw them later and explained what had been going on. 'When he gets the pain next month do we just send him off to school regardless?'

I told them that I didn't think that was the answer, pointing out that the pains their son was getting were undoubtedly very real.

'The answer,' I explained, 'is to try and stop him worrying so much about the spelling test.'

'Talk to him about it, help him to understand that as long as he does his best you won't mind what score he gets, ask his teacher to play down the importance of the test and gradually try to build up his confidence. Give him some small tests at home to get him used to them. And ask his teacher, too, to make it clear that anyone who misses the test will be expected to take it at some later date.'

That is exactly what they did. And I'm delighted to be able to say that it worked. William's mind learned that it would not be able to avoid the pressure of a school test by creating physical symptoms and it learned that the importance of the test was limited. William had been using an illness to help him cope with a real life problem, and the symptoms of his illness would undoubtedly have continued to puzzle us all if the surgeon hadn't spotted the link between the abdominal pains and the spelling tests.

In the years that followed I came across a great many other patients who were subconsciously using quite genuine physical problems to help them with problems in their daily lives. I met a young solicitor who used his migraines to help him avoid meeting a particularly objectionable client. I met an elderly lady who used her arthritis to enable her to avoid travelling with her sister. And I met a young woman who used her menstrual problems to help her avoid intercourse with a husband she no longer loved.

All these patients had allowed symptoms to develop and to grow in such a way that they provided them with an excuse for not doing something that they were frightened of or didn't want to do. And in every case it was quite impossible to treat the disease without finding out what benefit the patient was getting from it, and finding some alternative way to deal with the social or mental worry that was at the root of the problem.

If the surgeon hadn't spotted the link between young William's spelling tests and his abdominal pains then William would have undoubtedly lost his appendix and been treated with all sorts of drug therapies. His pains would not have gone away, however, because the original problem would have remained unchanged. And if I hadn't spotted that the solicitor was developing migraines when he had a particularly trouble-some client to see he would have carried on getting migraines whatever treatments had been tried.

To a certain extent we all use such excuses to avoid unpleasant tasks. A physical symptom or two can give us a solid, reliable excuse whenever we are embarrassed, fright-ened, nervous or ashamed. Getting a cold is a good way of avoiding a dinner party you don't fancy very much. Acquiring a mild muscle strain is an excellent way to get out of a sporting confrontation that you fear. And acquiring a headache is a classic way of avoiding an unwanted sexual encounter.

Some of the unconscious links between the body and the mind have drifted into the language. So, for example, we say things like: 'He is a pain in the neck', 'He makes me sick', 'They get up my nose', 'He makes me weak at the knees', 'I can't swallow that', 'I wish he'd get off my back', 'I've got cold feet' and 'I had to get it off my chest'.

If you are using symptoms or an illness as an excuse, you'll almost certainly be totally unaware of it. But if the link is there, it won't be difficult to find. And it will be well worth while doing the necessary digging, for using symptoms of ill health in this apparently advantageous way will, in the long run, produce far more problems than it solves. Your basic fear won't have disappeared. You will still be responding to stress in an unhealthy way. And you will have developed or exacerbated a condition which will have an adverse effect on your health and on your ability to enjoy life.

If you do suspect that you could be developing a set of symptoms in order to protect yourself from unpleasant or threatening experiences, you must ask yourself what benefits you gain from the illness and what the illness really means to you. Then you must learn to deal with your problems in a more positive and constructive way. Ask yourself what it is that you find so difficult to accept that you need to use an illness to hide from it. And then look for alternative solutions.

So, for example, if your back condition always seems to get a lot worse the day before your monthly Parent–Teachers Association Committee meeting, it might be more sensible for you to resign from the committee. You should, at the very least, ask yourself what it is that you dislike so much about these meetings.

If your migraine headaches become particularly incapacitating when you have to see your area manager then ask yourself what it is about the meetings that causes you so much distress. What are you frightened of? What is the worst that the area manager can do to you? Is the job worth the worry and the aggravation?

If your colitis always gets worse when you have particular jobs to do, the best way to treat the colitis will be either to find a way of avoiding those tasks or to try and find out what it is about those tasks that you find so impossible to accept.

If your child always develops a strange stomach ache on the third Tuesday of every month, find out what worries him about the third Tuesday of the month. What benefits does he get from his illness? What does the illness really mean to him?

If your partner always gets a headache when you make sexual overtures, ask yourself what is wrong with your relationship – not what you can do about the headaches. When your mind is using your body, the solution to your body's problem can be found by studying your mind.

Incidentally, there is one final thing that parents should remember: make sure that you don't overprotect children who are in pain and do not encourage children to associate pain with love and affection. Parents will often make a tremendous fuss of children when they bump themselves. The result is that the children grow up linking pain and discomfort to cuddling and care. In the long run that can easily lead to all sorts of problems.

Boredom

We tend to think of stress and pressure as being caused by too much activity. But inactivity and boredom can be just as great a cause of stress and can cause all the physical and mental problems associated with having too much to do.

There are four basic groups of people whose lives are threatened by boredom and inaction. First, there are those people whose daily work is undemanding and unrewarding. There are millions of people around today whose work demands nothing more than that they act as nursemaids to expensive, complicated pieces of machinery which they do not understand. In factories there are pieces of machinery which can turn out an endless stream of finely finished objects. No craftsman working with his own hands and tools could hope to emulate such accuracy. In offices there are computers and word processors which can write letters, check spelling and keep files far more speedily and efficiently than any individual could hope to do them. These days machines are so sophisticated that they are invariably the principals in any working relationship. The individual is left little opportunity for pride or self-expression.

Replacing skilled workmen with machines has led to a second major cause of boredom – unemployment. With remarkably short-sighted political approval, companies are installing more and more machinery and laying off an increasing proportion of their workforce. Unemployment produces a number of damaging forces, of which boredom is one of the most destructive.

The third group of individuals who suffer from boredom are those who have retired from work but who have too little to do in their later years. Thousands of men and women who have retired at fifty and fifty-five have then discovered that life without work can too often become dull, purposeless and boring.

Finally, boredom is a major cause of stress among the many women whose work keeps them in their homes. Tied to the kitchen sink and washing machine by a cluster of small

86

children, today's housewife can suffer enormously from boredom. There isn't a lot of opportunity for job satisfaction when you spend your days opening packets of cake mix and hunting for lost socks, only to find that no one respects and appreciates your achievements afterwards.

There have been countless reports published showing that people who are unemployed, or whose jobs are dull and unexciting, suffer from all the usual stress-related diseases. They have a much higher than average risk of developing stomach ulcers, heart disease, asthma and skin problems such as eczema. But the politicians and the journalists still underestimate the power of boredom as a force. They still fail to understand that it is boredom that is causing much of the stress-related disease in our society. And they fail to see that it is often boredom that drives people to drugs or alcohol. The housewife who becomes a secret drinker, the schoolboy who starts sniffing glue, the pensioner who takes too many tranquillizers, the football vandal who behaves in a violent and inexcusable way all have one thing in common: their lives are dull, monotonous, unexciting and without hope. There seems to be no escape from the daily boredom and no hope for the future.

Under the circumstances, it is not surprising that there is so much violence on our football terraces and so much drug-taking in our streets. It is, rather, surprising that there is so little.

Anyone suffering from boredom – or the ill effects of boredom – needs to add excitement to his or her life. Excitement can provide a stimulus that can keep the mind and the body active and healthy.

Tony, Robert and Chris were all patients in a hospital where the matron had a reputation for being more like a prison camp warder than a hospital administrator. They were kept under close control by a small army of warders dressed as nurses. All three men had had fairly minor surgical operations but they were all taking an awfully long time to get better. They were bored out of their minds. They weren't allowed to get out of bed for more than ten minutes at a time. They weren't allowed to talk to one another in anything louder than a whisper. And they certainly weren't allowed to play cards.

I think that they might well have still been in the hospital to this day – still convalescing – if they hadn't decided to rebel and add a touch of excitement to their lives. Over a period of two or three days they carefully planned a break-out. They knew that there was a pub about fifty yards away from the hospital entrance and so they set about planning a late-night drinking trip. They got relatives to smuggle in outdoor clothes and they hid these clothes underneath their mattresses. They practised making body-sized lumps out of pillows and bolsters. They found a loose window in the bathroom through which they could escape to the street. And they even planned a minor diversion in a side ward.

And it worked. They managed to get out of the hospital for twenty minutes and drink half a pint of lager each. And they managed to get back into bed without anyone noticing. But the excitement that was built up by planning and executing the expedition did them – and the rest of the ward – a tremendous amount of good. Forty-eight hours after their escape the three of them were discharged and allowed to go back home.

If you feel that parts of your life are unspeakably dull and that you need to balance that boredom by adding excitement and colour to your life, do not despair. There are plenty of ways in which you can add excitement to your life.

1   Take up a pastime or hobby which you find rewarding. Do something that you can become really good at, and something that you can take pride in. If you have no job at all then consider the possibility of establishing a small business of your own. Window cleaning, grass cutting, gardening and catering for special events are just a few of the obvious ways to begin a small business venture without much capital.

2   If you find yourself working with machines which you don't understand, and which break down regularly, do your best to find out how they operate and how you can keep them going. Ask for instruction manuals and read them. Write to the manufacturers for background information and for any details that aren't included in the service manual.

If you spend your days with a machine which you don't understand, it will become your master and ruin your life. If you know how the machine works and you can help keep it in good working condition then it can become your servant.

3   If you need more intellectual stimulation in your life, or you feel the need for new friends, then start taking evening

classes or day classes at a local college. Don't just pick a subject that sounds useful. Find something that excites you and that you will enjoy. If it's useful as well, consider that a bonus.

4   Learn to avoid potentially boring situations with as much skill and tact as you can muster.

A friend of mine who works in television has an excellent technique for avoiding boring meetings. He explains that he feels overloaded with information, agrees that the subject is an important one, argues that he needs time to think about it before discussing it further and disappears to 'think' about the subject in silent privacy. He says all this with charm and sincerity and I've never yet seen it fail him.

5   Plan your life as cautiously as you like and as carefully as you can. But be prepared to take risks occasionally. If you never take risks because you are frightened of the possible consequences, your life will be dull. The individuals whose lives we find most attractive are often those who are most readily prepared to take chances. In the world of sport we tend to admire people like Franz Klammer, the skier, the late Gilles Villeneuve, the racing driver, Ian Botham, the cricketer, George Best, the footballer and Alex 'Hurricane' Higgins, the snooker player. We find their daring and courage exciting and attractive. They fail quite often, but their attitude to life means that they are never dull to watch and their lives are never boring.

If you take risks and fail, you will at least have tried. If you never take risks, you'll never know what you could have achieved. And you'll probably die of boredom. What a sad way to go.

6   If you are doing something immeasurably dull and un-speakably boring, escape by creating a fantasy daydream for yourself. Think of a situation that you would enjoy, of people you would like to be with, and of places you would like to visit. Then add as much exotic (or erotic) background to the fantasy as you like. This type of daydream is quite different from the type of daydream needed for relaxation. In order to relax your mind you need to create a soothing, calm, relaxing situation. In order to defeat boredom you need an invigorating, exciting fantasy.

Fantasize about success, about what you would do if you won half a million pounds on the football pools, about what it would be like to have a motor yacht moored at Monaco, about what it would be like to trek across the Himalayas.

If you have difficulty in creating suitable fantasies for yourself, collect a pile of brochures from a travel agent or buy one or two glossy magazines from your newsagents. A journal full of pictures of elegant country houses, expensive boats or naked women should provide a useful starting point.

This type of simple but rewarding fantasy will help provide you with a temporary escape from your boredom. But by providing you with a positive approach to your life and by filling your mind with positive, pleasant images, it will also improve your confidence and self-assurance.

Failing relationships

Our relationships with other people have a tremendous influence on our lives in general and our health in particular. When close relationships founder or crumble altogether, we often respond badly to stresses and strains that might ordinarily be regarded as relatively insignificant. Arguments with loved ones, with colleagues at work and with friends can cause a wide range of emotional responses. In order to stay healthy it is clearly important that we understand what factors influence how we get on with other people.

The first thing to realize is that our own attitudes do not stay constant. We all behave in many different ways when we are with different people. We act differently with our lovers, employers, employees, spouses, neighbours, doctors, friends, parents and children.

A middle-aged, divorced man working as a highly placed business executive may be bitter towards his ex-wife, sycophantic towards the chairman of his company, lustful towards his young, blonde secretary, respectful towards his parents, tyrannical towards his assistants and domineering with his children. In return, his parents may be proud of him, his secretary may be embarrassed and offended by his unwanted advances, his wife may be jealous of his freedom, his children may fear him, his chairman may despise him and his assistants may simply dislike him.

However stable and constant we may consider ourselves,

different people will always think of us in different ways. Our bank managers don't see us in the same way that our neighbours do. The friends we go on holiday with won't see the same side of us as the people we work with.

Our roles in life will vary according to our own beliefs and aspirations, according to the attitudes and needs of others and according to the ways in which our needs and their needs interreact. We are none of us single individuals. If our parents described our virtues our business enemies would not recognize us. If our children described us, the chances are that our employers wouldn't know whom they were talking about.

Yet we tend to jump to instant conclusions about other people and about the way other people see us. We make assumptions which may prove damaging or destructive. We spend remarkably little time thinking about our relationships with other people. It is, in the end, hardly surprising that our relationships with others often break down and produce great heartache and distress. It is hardly surprising, indeed, that instead of being a source of comfort, our close relationships with other people are often a source of great unhappiness and subsequent physical illness.

The questionnaire on pages 151–2 is designed to help you assess the strengths and weaknesses of all your personal relationships. If you try to understand the basis upon which your relationships are built, you will be much more likely to enjoy those relationships rather than suffer through them.

There are, however, some simple, basic guidelines worth following with all your relationships.

1 Try to take care not to allow the prejudices of others to influence your attitudes to people you have not met. If you accept other people's judgements, you will often make mistakes. Remember that any relationship is a result of an interaction between two quite separate sets of needs, ambitions and requirements. If you accept second-hand judgements, you are accepting second-hand needs, ambitions and requirements.

2 When you meet someone new, try not to allow your past prejudices and personal experiences to have too much influence on your relationships. If you judge people by the way they dress, for example, you will only ever make friends with people who have a similar social or cultural background to

yourself. Read also the notes on page 69 which describe how past associations can influence relationships.

3   Always remember that even people who are close to you will often have feelings, ambitions and fears which vary considerably from your own. Consequently their attitudes towards specific events may also vary considerably from yours.

If you expect other people to respond to varying circumstances in the same way as you, you will undoubtedly end up being disappointed. Try to learn as much as you can about the people with whom you have close relationships – the people who are important to you and your health. And try to understand their fears and needs. If you do this, your personal relationships will be strengthened.

Guilt

Guilt is an emotion that is as common as love and as damaging as hate. It is an emotion that is difficult to define precisely, but in practical terms it is hard to distinguish it from what we commonly call our consciences. We feel guilty when we have done something wrong – or not done something that we feel we ought to have done – because we feel that we have failed in some way. We torture ourselves with self-recriminations and then, having prosecuted ourselves, we find ourselves guilty. Guilt is one of the most powerful and damaging of human emotions. And, ironically, it is an emotion that is built on love and compassion.

There are so many possible sources of guilt that it is impossible to classify them all. But most varieties of guilt fall into one of two main categories. First, there are the types of guilt that result from our personal relationships with other people. Sometimes, guilt can be introduced crudely and deliberately, as when a mother says to her son or daughter, 'You wouldn't do that if you loved me'. Sometimes, guilt is produced subtly and unintentionally, as when one partner says to another, 'Don't worry about me, you go off and enjoy yourself. I'll be all right.'

There are other types of guilt which result from the demands, expectations and teachings of those around us.

Most of us have an inbuilt sense of right and wrong and if we trespass against it, we feel guilty. This inbuilt sense of right and wrong does not, however, come from some mysterious, inherited force, but from social and religious prejudices which have been established by instruction and example. Some of these forces are sound, logical and simple – so, for example, most of us feel guilty if we steal, because stealing is widely considered to be an anti-social activity. But other feelings of guilt are not so easy to explain, developing as they do from prejudices and fears which do not have such obvious origins. So, we feel guilty if we lie in bed on Sunday morning, if we earn too much money, if we allow ourselves to be seen naked on the beach or if we enjoy ourselves too much. These types of guilt are produced by pressures exerted by teachers, religious leaders, politicians, philosophers and pundits of all kinds.

All this guilt has a number of damaging effects on the way we live. But the most important and damaging effect it has is to create within us a feeling of inferiority and inadequacy: a positive lack of self-confidence. We feel guilty because we fail to live up to the expectations of those around us (both personal and social) and as a result we feel insecure and lose our confidence.

It is directly through its ability to damage our confidence that guilt causes so much physical and mental damage. Because we feel guilty about our failure to satisfy our parents (and others who have expectations for us) we feel a sense of shame and we lose our self-esteem. And as a result we push ourselves far more cruelly than any slave driver ever pushed his slave.

This internally inspired pressure is the most damaging type of stress. It is impossible to escape from it and the consequences can be far-reaching. The greater our lack of self-confidence, the greater our risk of developing heart disease, stomach ulcers, asthma, intestinal problems, skin conditions and the other hundred and one problems associated with pressure and tension.

So, for example, the workaholic who cannot relax and who must force himself to continue working, even though he has all the money he is ever likely to need, continues to work harder and harder. This may be because he has no self-confidence, because he has no self-esteem, because he still fears failure, because he desperately needs to please those whose respect he yearns for, or because whatever he does, however great his achievements may be, he has a continuing sense of inadequacy. All those feelings will have very probably been inspired by his continuing failure to elicit praise from his parents. His duodenal ulcer, his raised blood pressure and his heart condition will all have been produced by the guilt he feels at failing their expectations.

If your health is being put at risk by a lack of self-confidence, you can use your mind to help your body by emptying it of hate, regret, fear and guilt and filling it instead with positive feelings and hopeful thoughts; you must learn to think of yourself as a success.

There are ten specific steps that you can take to help yourself conquer guilt and gain health-giving confidence.

1   If you lack confidence, the chances are that, although you know very well what your weaknesses are, you don't know what your strengths are. You are probably rather timid and shy (even though other people may not realize that) and you doubtless have little faith in your own abilities.

To counteract those fears, sit yourself down with a piece of paper and a pencil and write down all the good things you can think of to say about yourself. Imagine that you're preparing your own obituary and try to pick out all your very best points. You'll probably be amazed to see just how many virtues you have got. Individuals who are shy and lacking in self-confidence tend to be unusually honest, generous, thoughtful and hard-working. You're probably punctual, careful, moral, kind, ambitious and unusually creative.

Alternatively, try writing an advertisement for yourself. Pretend that you are a copywriter with the job of selling yourself to a group of potential 'buyers'. Write a piece of advertising copy extolling your virtues, outlining all your good points and exaggerating all your advantages. Remember to list all your physical as well as mental attributes. Study your advertisement as often as you can in order to build up your own image of yourself.

2   Learn to put things into proportion. You may feel that you have failed your parents because you haven't managed to become a millionaire by the age of thirty-five but would you really criticize anyone else for such an absurd 'failure'? You'll

almost certainly find that you expect far too much from yourself – and put yourself under quite unreasonable amounts of pressure. The section on 'priorities', pages 107–110. examines how we can put our problems in perspective.

3   Try to boost your self-confidence by thinking of your faults as virtues. Shyness, for example, isn't necessarily a disadvantage. The unusually shy are often exceptionally aware of the needs of others and well aware of the problems involved in building up any sort of relationship. The shy tend to try harder – and have greater amounts of care and unselfish affection to share with their friends and loved ones.

You may be rather obsessional. But that probably means that you pay great attention to detail and that you can be relied upon to be observant and watchful. You're probably often unusually sensitive to criticism. And yet just think of those individuals who are insensitive to criticism: they can often be rude, unthinking and boorish. Which would you rather be?

4   Your lack of self-confidence will mean that you will often worry about disastrous things happening to you. It may be possible for you to 'defuse' this particular fear by always asking yourself, 'What is the worst thing that can happen in this situation?' You'll often be surprised to find that the 'worst' really isn't all that bad. Once you know the worst, you can make plans accordingly.

When taking examinations at school and medical school I, like just about everyone I know, used to worry about what would happen if I failed. But when I stopped to think about it, I realized that it really wasn't all that terrible. It would have simply meant that I'd have had to change courses or get a job. I would have still have had my health and plenty of opportunities to enjoy my life. It didn't take much imagination to convince myself that failing would probably mean that I'd be able to have much more fun. When I stopped worrying so much about the examinations and had removed the fear of the unknown (the most potent fear in the world) I found them far less of a threat and far less of a problem.

You can use this same sort of technique in all sorts of situations where you feel shy or nervous. For example, if you want to ask your boss for a raise, but you feel frightened about what will happen if he says 'no', just ask yourself what is the worst possible consequence of your confronting him. You'll probably decide that the worst thing that can happen is that he'll sack you for having such an outrageous cheek. But will that really be such a terrible thing? If you are so badly underpaid that you've got to ask for a raise, and your boss is so unreasonable that he's likely to sack you for asking for one, wouldn't you be better off trying your luck elsewhere?

5   Try not to think of every rejection as a personal insult. If the film producers who read the play you have written all send it back, it may very well be because they are busy with some other project, or because they don't have the intelligence to spot a winner when they see one. They aren't turning it down because they hate you or your script.

6   When you are next feeling rather down, make a list of all your assets. I don't mean a bald list of the money you've got and the things you own, but a list of the things in your life that are important to you – your partner, your children, your integrity, your friends, your health, your country, your interests, your knowledge, your accomplishments and so on.

7   Make a list of all the things you are supposed to be really bad at. Then put the list in order, your worst shortcomings at the top of the list. Then work your way up the list from the bottom, doing what you can to eradicate each shortcoming in turn.

We all get labels as we go through life and those labels are often quite unfair. If you've put up a shelf and its been crooked, you'll have probably acquired a label as a useless handyman. And yet if you were given another chance, you would probably be able to show that you had learned from your mistakes. If you didn't like gardening when you were small and were told to weed what looked like a forty-acre patch, you'll probably grow up with a reputation as someone who isn't any good at gardening. In fact, you may be quite good at gardening. And it may be something that you'd really enjoy.

Labels can often be applied on the basis of an isolated comment or experience or a misinterpretation. But once you have acquired a label, you'll find yourself expecting to fail. Because of other people's feelings about you, you will have learned to he helpless and incompetent.

8   Try to be aware that there are many people who have a vested interest in your shortcomings. Manufacturers and

advertisers want you to think that you are incompetent so that they call sell you products to help give you confidence. Colleagues and rivals want you to feel incompetent so that they can improve their own status and standing. And, occasionally, friends and relatives will want you to feel incompetent so that they can continue to boost their own confidence by providing you with guidance and protection.

9 Don't be ashamed of your mistakes. Everyone makes mistakes occasionally. Don't worry about admitting that you are wrong. No one can be right all the time. Accept your responsibility, deal with any consequences and try to learn what you can from the error. Other people who find it difficult to accept your apologies are very probably short of confidence themselves. They are particularly conscious of your errors because you remind them of their own fallibility.

10 Accept your limitations, your shortcomings and your faults. Find out just how far you are prepared to go – and how far you won't go. Then temper this knowledge of your limitations with the realization that everyone else has limitations too. But at least you know what yours are. And that will always give you an edge.

CHAPTER 6

Using your mind to heal your body – controlling positive forces

Laughter

The story of the man who laughed himself back to good health is now well known. Norman Cousins had been assured by his doctors that there was no cure for the inflammatory disease that was crippling him. The physicians had, sadly, told Norman that all they could do was to try to keep him comfortable. Desperately unhappy about the prognosis and feeling extremely miserable in his dreary hospital room, Norman Cousins moved out and went to stay in a nearby hotel. There he deliberately tried to cheer himself up by watching some of his favourite comedy films and reading books by some of his favourite writers of humour.

Not only did Norman find that he felt better in his happy hotel room than he had felt in his hospital room, but with the aid of the doctors who were still looking after him, he managed to produce incontrovertible scientific evidence to show that his laughter and his merriment had had a useful, positive, practical effect on his physical condition. The hospital laboratory even showed that there had been a reduction in the inflammatory changes affecting his body. Norman Cousins had laughed himself better.

Just how laughter and humour can have such a positive effect on the human body is still something of a mystery. It has been suggested that laughter helps by improving respiration, by lowering the blood pressure and, possibly, by increasing the supply of specific types of internally produced healing hormone. The diaphragm is relaxed, the lungs are exercised (with the result that the amount of oxygen in the blood is increased) and the cardiovascular system is given a good tuning-up exercise.

Dr Paul Ekman of the University of California has claimed that the very act of flexing the facial muscles into a smile may produce a genuine and calming effect on the nervous system, heart rate and respiratory system. Next time you're feeling miserable just try putting a really cheerful smile on your face. You'll find it difficult to stay quite so sad. Try making your eyes sparkle with laughter and you'll notice the effect even more.

Humour also helps by diverting the patient's attention. When you're busy laughing at something that you're reading or watching, you 'forget' that you have a pain. When I worked as a hospital doctor we always used to have a Christmas pantomime for the younger patients. And the number of pain killers that we had to dish out on the day of the pantomime was always very low. Laughter isn't just a pleasant experience. It is a positive, natural phenomenon which helps to ensure that the body benefits to the fullest extent. It may well be that laughter really is the best medicine!

There are a number of things that you can do to help put more laughter into your life. First, you can try to spend as much time as possible with cheerful, happy people. If you spend your days with people who always have long faces and always look on the black side, the chances are that eventually you will acquire a long face and a gloomy view of life. Depression is contagious. Psychiatrists do a lot of silly things, but it has always struck me that the silliest thing they do is put all their depressed patients together on a ward. Spend as much time as possible with people who laugh and enjoy life to the full. You will benefit from their company. Bright and cheerful friends will probably do you far more good than any pills your doctor can prescribe.

Second, try not to take yourself too seriously. Many people with reasonably responsible jobs feel that they have to maintain a serious demeanour at all times. And yet they're quite wrong. As long as you take care to preserve your serious manner for the times when it really matters, you'll lose nothing by allowing yourself to laugh occasionally.

A patient of mine who had a job as a factory foreman always

suffered from terrible headaches when he was at work – largely because he took himself and his responsibility far too seriously. He never got headaches when he was on holiday, enjoying himself with his family and friends. When I managed to persuade him to take his role in life a little less seriously and to have a bit more fun at work he found that his headaches stopped troubling him. And, even more to his surprise, he found that the people working for him respected him just as much. The bonus was that they liked him as well.

Third, make a list now of your favourite funny films and books. If you have a video recorder try to keep copies of one or two films that you find particularly pleasing – and that you know you can rely on to provide you with an hour or two of genuine relaxation. And keep a library of your favourite funny books. When you find a favourite author whose books always amuse you, keep one or two of his or her books on one side for a bad day when you need to cheer yourself up. I've always got half a dozen light novels and books of cartoons on one side of my desk. I know that if I feel a bit low I can always find something there to cheer me up quickly. The funny thing is, of course, that when you know that you've got something that you can rely on to cheer you up a little, you hardly ever need it. Just having a tonic to pick up and read is enough.

Of course, if you don't like books, magazines or comics can give you good laughs. I recently met a man with a very responsible job in banking who always keeps a copy of a boy's comic in his briefcase. If he's had a particular hard day at the bank, he gets it out to read on the train back home. He used to hide it behind a copy of *The Times*. These days he doesn't care who sees him reading it.

We can't always lift ourselves out of the slough of a cruelly destructive despair by watching funny films or reading funny books. When things are really bad, we often rely on the understanding of friends and relatives. Sadly, very few people visiting sick friends or relatives offer much in the way of positive encouragement through laughter. The average visitor turns up at the bedside clutching a brown paper bag full of grapes (which the patient never normally eats and doesn't like very much anyway) and then sits for half an hour or so offering an uninspiring series of sorry anecdotes and dreary gossip. It's really hardly surprising that when the average visitor leaves

100

the average bedside, the average patient is more miserable and depressed than ever.

If, on the other hand, visitors were to arrive at the hospital or bedside with a bag full of cheerful magazines and lively books and half an hour's worth of jolly stories and merry jokes, the patient would be much happier and much more cheerful on their departure. Smiles are as contagious as yawns and even the slightest of grins or the weakest of laughs can have a beneficial healing effect.

The value of keeping patients cheerful and happy is now so well established that hospital authorities should pay more attention to the ways in which they could make patients happy. There are many experts around the world who now claim that doctors can do more for the health of their patients by helping them to laugh and smile than by encouraging them to lose weight, give up smoking or watch what they eat. Whatever the truth of that, there seems to me to be little doubt that we should all pay more attention to the value of the healing smile. Every effort should be made to make hospitals warm and friendly places and to ensure that staff members recognize the importance of trying to keep patients entertained and happy.

Purpose

I don't remember much that I learned while studying chemistry at school, but one thing does stick in my mind. We were studying the freezing points of gases when the chemistry master told us a rather sad story about the man who had dedicated his life to identifying these scientific landmarks. After working in his laboratory for many years, the scientist eventually managed to complete his research; he found the freezing point of the last remaining gas. His wife and his colleagues thought that he would be overwhelmed with joy. He had completed his life's work and achieved more than most ordinary men could ever hope to achieve. But the scientist wasn't overcome with joy. On the contrary, he was plunged into the very depths of despair. He became severely depressed and within a month or two of making his final, momentous discovery he was dead. Once his life's work was finished, there was nothing left for him to live for.

101

I've heard of men who have retired, come home, hung up their work boots, gone to bed and never woken up again. I've heard of explorers who have been plunged into the very depths of despair after finishing adventures that should have killed them, but which kept them alive for years. I've heard of mountaineers being overcome with misery after conquering mountains that had defied them for decades. I've heard of sportsmen and women wandering about as though lost and in despair after winning trophies they had yearned for since childhood.

The truth is, of course, that we do all need a purpose in our lives. We need something to hope for, something to fight for and something to look forward to. Without purpose and meaning our lives are hollow and unrewarding. With purpose and hope we can survive the meanest of circumstances and the most distressing of problems. Purpose and ambition enable us to live through the worst of life's crises.

Begin putting purpose into your life by making a list of all the goals and ambitions that you had when you were a teenager. Try to think back and remember what hopes and aspirations fired your imagination at that age. Perhaps you dreamt of becoming an actor, a musician, a politician or an artist. Include all your ambitions on your list – long-term as well as short-term ones, reasonable expectations alongside outrageous, wild dreams.

Then take a look through your list to see just how many of those dreams and ambitions still excite you. Forget your responsibilities and commitments for a few moments and try to revive and relive your teenage hopes and enthusiasms. Remember the talents you felt that you had and the energy that gave your life meaning.

Now think carefully about your ambitions and hopes and you'll probably realize that a number of your old dreams are still possible. You may be too old to become a world gymnastic champion, but you aren't too old to write a book or a play. Your dream of becoming an astronaut may seem a little far-fetched now, but your plan to travel around the world need not be impossible. By repressing and forgetting your hopes and your ambitions, you will have reduced any likelihood of them being realized. If you dismiss a dream as impossible, your negative attitude will influence your approach – and will influence the attitude of others who might have been able to help you. Remove those unnecessary restrictions and your subconscious mind will spring to your help. Once you decide that you would like to take up painting (and that there really isn't anything to stop you taking up painting) you'll start to notice all sorts of hints and tips and possibilities that you would otherwise have missed.

If someone mentions a well-known actor whom you've never heard of before, then the chances are that you'll see the actor's name everywhere you look for the next few days. Your enhanced awareness means that you notice things that you would otherwise have missed. Similarly, by allowing your hidden ambitions to surface, you'll enable your mind to help you collect useful bits and pieces of information. So, if you decide that you really would still like to take up painting, you'll notice an advertisement in your local paper announcing that new evening classes are about to start, you'll notice an article in your favourite magazine giving rudimentary advice about sketching equipment and you'll hear people talking about art exhibitions for beginners. Without doing anything other than recognize your own ambition (and thereby put purpose into your life), you will have greatly improved your chances of realizing that ambition.

The main advantage will be that your life will have been given a fresh purpose and a new meaning. Without ambitions and hopes and aspirations our lives are sterile and empty. With them you will have given yourself tremendous new powers with which to combat the stresses and strains associated with your daily boredom, pressures and frustrations.

Whatever your age, your job and your personal responsibilities, your life needs purpose and direction as much as it needs food and oxygen. You need to be stretched, you need to take chances and you need to know that, whatever you may achieve, you have at least given yourself every chance of satisfying those early ambitions and dreams.

Optimism

When I was in my final year at medical school just about

everyone I knew seemed to be heading for a nervous break-down. After five years of study our nerves had become rather frayed. Two of the students with whom I worked reacted to this pressure in very different ways.

Jack was extremely pessimistic about it all. He had studied carefully and conscientiously and knew just about everything he needed to know. He was one of the best students in my year and he was almost certain to pass. In spite of this, he seemed convinced that he would fail. He spent his days reading textbooks and moping around the flat in a terrible state of despair.

Christopher, on the other hand, was wildly optimistic. He had spent hardly any time studying and had already failed several examinations. He had been warned by the Dean on several occasions, but he had a very happy-go-lucky attitude. He was convinced that he would pass. And not particularly worried about what would happen if he didn't.

When the examination results were posted, Jack had passed (although he hadn't done quite as well as the rest of us had thought he would do), but Christopher had failed. You might have thought that Jack would have been pleased with himself and would have rushed off to celebrate his success. But you'd be wrong. He wasn't pleased and he didn't go and celebrate. With one problem out of the way he started worrying about another hurdle: getting a prestigious hospital job. He told anyone who would listen that it was vitally important to get the right sort of job in the right sort of hospital in exactly the right sort of area, and that he knew for a fact that if he didn't get the right post his career would be in ruins.

Christopher, on the other hand, was remarkably calm about his failure. He seemed to take it all in his stride, happily looking foward to another few months as a carefree medical student. 'It'll be a peaceful six months,' he insisted, 'and it'll mean that I can delay paying income tax for another six months of my life.'

Jack was an absolutely typical pessimist: always thinking that the worst was about to happen and always prepared for disaster. Christopher, on the other hand, was an incorrigible optimist. He never really allowed himself to worry about things.

After we left medical school I lost contact with both of them.

Recently, out of curiosity, I got in touch. Jack is working as a leading hospital consultant in a very pleasant part of the country. But when I spoke to him he was worried about the fact that he doesn't have a very good pension plan to look foward to. He was also worried about his daughter, who is due to start taking important school examinations shortly. He is convinced that she will fail and make a disaster of her life. He also confessed to being worried about his raised blood pressure and about the fact that he has already had a number of niggling chest pains.

Christopher is working as a general practitioner in a busy inner city practice and sounds as carefree and optimistic as ever. He plays golf a couple of times a week, has a small touring caravan which he and his family tow around France for several weeks every summer and enjoys more or less perfect health.

These two doctors seem to me to illustrate very accurately the simple difference between an optimist and a pessimist. Jack is always worrying about something. He can never enjoy the good things in his life because he is always worrying about the things that are likely to go wrong. He already has one or two serious health problems and if I were representing an insurance company, I wouldn't be too happy about selling him a life insurance policy. Christopher, on the other hand, is a perpetual optimist. Whatever life throws at him he will never stop smiling or looking on the bright side. He will probably live for ever.

If you look around among your friends, relatives and neighbours, you'll probably find that most of the people you know are neither exceptionally optimistic nor exceptionally pessimistic. But you will find that most people do tend to be either largely one type or the other. And you'll find too that the people who are mainly pessimistic tend, on the whole, to suffer more with their health than the individuals who are more optimistic.

If you are a naturally pessimistic individual then it would not be easy to convert yourself into a full-blown optimist. But it will be possible to temper your pessimism with some optimism. Try first of all to start each day in a cheerful, optimistic frame of mind. If you get up in the morning thinking of all the terrible chores you've got to do, and the awful people you have to meet, it won't take much to turn a potentially horrendous day into a truly awful experience.

If something goes wrong early on in the day, your attitude will simply make things worse. Your gloom will deepen and your approach will probably mean that one disaster will follow another. As you wander around with your scowl and your gloomy demeanour the people you meet will be depressed by your approach. It won't be surprising if they respond accordingly. And by evening you'll be in a deep, dark depression of your own. Your pessimism will have rebounded on you and rebuilt your own fear and misery. Your depression, confusion, fear, anger and frustration will together end up producing genuine physical symptoms of disease.

When you get up try to think of all the good things that make your life worth living. Do you have the use of all your limbs and your eyes? Do you have a partner who cares for you? Do you have children who love and need you? Do you have things to look forward to in the future – a holiday or a weekend away or a party? Do you have a good book you're looking forward to reading? A television programme you're planning to watch? A sporting encounter that you're looking forward to? A meeting with friends?

Take pleasure in the small things in your life: the clean shirt, the first cup of tea or coffee in the morning, the birds in the garden, the smell of rain and so on. Think of the chores that you have in front of you as single tasks to be undertaken. Think of the worst of them as a challenge to your good humour – to be tackled with determination and enthusiasm.

Every job that has to be done can be looked at in a variety of different ways. A man laying bricks can think of himself as having a dull, tedious job that merely involves placing one brick next to another for hours on end. Or he can think of himself as earning a living for himself and his family so that they can live together as comfortably and as happily as possible. Or he can think of himself as helping to create a house which some new family will excitedly turn into a home.

Try to establish a positive approach to everything you do and everyone you meet. Although you will sometimes be disappointed, you will gain far more from your life than if you constantly nurture a cautious, negative approach.

If you buy a new car, 'discover' a new holiday resort or hear about a new film star, the chances are that for the next few days or weeks you will see and hear nothing else but the name of the type of car you've bought, the place you've discovered or the star you've found. Your interest and your memory will enhance your sense of awareness.

Through a similar sort of mental mechanism your interests and your memories will dominate your attitudes to other things in your life. If you have an unhappy experience when trying to put up a shelf, your impressions and memories of your skills with a hammer and a piece of wood will be negative. If you make a mistake in a business deal, you will be unusually cautious when you are in similar situations. If a relationship fails, you will remember that failure when trying to develop new relationships. Your attitudes and your memories will affect your responses and your approach to fresh encounters.

When things go wrong, as they most surely will in anyone's life, you should try to learn what you can from each unhappy experience and then forget about it. You should extract what useful memories you can from each experience, and regard the experience as a lesson not a punishment. If you brood on your failures, the chances are that they will recur, eventually growing in your mind until they reach exaggerated and unmanageable proportions. Pessimists tend to think of their failures as unforgivable and eternally damning, whereas in truth they are priceless experiences without which none of us could change, progress or improve ourselves.

I'm not suggesting that failure is ever welcome, of course. But if you fear failure, as many pessimists do, then you will never try new projects. You should learn to dominate your failures by sharing them rather than hiding them, and by using them rather than by allowing them to limit you.

Assertiveness

Anne Bambridge came to my surgery about six weeks before Christmas. I can remember her visit vividly. I had only ever seen her before when she'd come to the surgery to collect a prescription for her contraceptive pill, or when she'd come in with one of her small children. But this time it wasn't one of the children who was ill. And she didn't need any more contraceptive pills.

'I'm in a terrible state, doctor,' she told me. 'Can you give me something to help me relax?'

Now in the weeks before Christmas just about everyone I know gets over-excited and rather anxious. There are so many things to be done – particularly if there are small children in the house – that a little tension is almost inevitable. So, I wasn't all that surprised by Mrs Bambridge's comment, even though Christmas was still quite a time away. I simply asked her to tell me what it was that was worrying her.

To my surprise she started to cry. Eventually, two or three paper handkerchiefs later, she managed to talk to me. She explained that she was worried and upset because her parents were coming to stay and she didn't think that she could cope.

'It's not the cooking or anything like that,' she explained quickly. 'It's just that they treat me like such an idiot and they push me around so much that I feel terrible. I get so angry with them and yet I never say anything to them, so I just get awfully frustrated.'

She went on to tell me that she invariably ended up with a more or less continuous headache for the whole of the Christmas holiday.

'Last year I got terrible colicky pains as well,' she confessed. 'And I'm sure that it's all just because I get so furious with myself for letting them come into my home and treat me the way they do.'

'What sort of things happen?' I asked her.

'Well, we like to watch some of the television programmes that are on over Christmas,' said Mrs Bambridge. 'But my mother doesn't think it's right to watch television at Christmas time so we all have to sit around and talk to one another. That would be all right if we could have a nice friendly natter, but it always ends up with my Dad moaning at Michael – that's my husband – for not having a better job and earning more money.'

'Sounds as if you have a pretty miserable time,' I agreed.

'And then on Boxing Day my father always insists that we go for a five-mile walk,' said Mrs Bambridge. 'He gets us all up early even though it's one of the few mornings in the year that Michael and I can have a bit of a lie in together.'

'Haven't you ever pointed out that you'd rather lie in bed while they go for a walk?' I asked her.

'I said that last year,' said Mrs Bambridge, 'and it took me all my courage to say it. But my father just laughed it off and said that I wasn't to be so silly, that a walk would do us good and so on.'

'And you gave in?'

'I don't like arguing,' said Mrs Bambridge. 'So I did give in. Then afterwards I felt really cross with myself. Do you know, I was ill for nearly a fortnight after they'd eventually gone home.'

'I gather that you'd really rather spend Christmas without your parents visiting?'

'Oh, it would be wonderful,' admitted Mrs Bambridge.

'Have you told your parents that you and your husband would like to have a quiet Christmas occasionally?'

'I half mentioned it a couple of years ago,' said Mrs Bambridge. 'But my mother got very nasty about it. She said that she thought it was very selfish of me to want to keep them away and pointed out that they always look forward to sharing their Christmas with us. She told me that if they didn't come to us, they'd have to stay at home by themselves and since there were only the two of them they wouldn't even be able to have a turkey. She made me feel really awful and I didn't say anything else about it.'

I explained to Mrs Bambridge that there wasn't much point in my simply giving her pills to turn her into a zombie over Christmas.

'Christmas is still six weeks away,' I pointed out, 'and you're in an absolutely terrible state already. What do you think you're going to be like by Christmas Eve? You'll be lucky if you're still on your own feet and not flat on your back in a hospital bed. Or in a straight jacket.'

Mrs Bambridge nodded in dumb agreement.

'But what can I do?' she demanded after a moment or two's silence. 'I couldn't tell them not to come. I'd feel awful.'

'Why would you feel awful?' I asked her.

'I'd feel I was letting them down,' Mrs Bambridge explained. 'I'd feel that I was just behaving selfishly.'

'From an outsider's point of view it looks to me as if it's your parents who have been behaving selfishly,' I told her. 'They're the ones who have insisted on sharing your Christmas and then organizing it the way that they want it organized.'

Mrs Bambridge thought for a moment and slowly nodded. 'They have been very unreasonable,' she agreed.

'If you had a good friend whose parents behaved in the same sort of way what would you tell her to do?'

'I'd suggest that she told her parents to do something else for once,' said Mrs Bambridge.

'You wouldn't think that she was behaving unreasonably or selfishly?'

'Not at all,' replied Mrs Bambridge straight away.

'Then if you're going to enjoy your Christmas and stay healthy you have to follow the same advice that you'd give to a good friend,' I told her. 'You've already admitted that you wouldn't think a friend who behaved like that would be behaving unreasonably.'

'How about if I said that one of the children wasn't well?' suggested Mrs Bambridge.

'What would your mother say?' I asked her.

'She'd probably insist on coming to make sure that I was looking after them properly,' Mrs Bambridge admitted.

'Exactly,' I agreed. 'There isn't much point in trying to offer excuses. Your parents won't be put off that easily. The only solution is to be entirely honest with them. You have to explain that you've thought about it long and hard and decided that this year you want to spend Christmas alone.'

'But what do I do when my mother starts on about the fact they'll be all alone too?'

'Tell her that it'll probably be nice for her and your father to share a Christmas without having to put up with all your noise, without your television set blaring and without having to drag you out of bed. And then fix a date now to see them after the holiday.'

'She'll be terribly offended.'

'And she'll get over it,' I promised. 'She may sulk for a while, but she'll get over it.'

There are thousands of people who, like my patient Mrs Bambridge, suffer enormously because of their inability to assert themselves. They are pushed around by parents, family, friends, relatives, employers, doctors and just about everyone else they meet. Their lives are run by others. They find themselves doing errands for people who could perfectly well run their own errands. They find themselves sitting on committees and doing boring administrative jobs which no one else wants. They find themselves lumbered with looking after the children while everyone else goes off to have a good time at a party. They find themselves working overtime at the weekends and not getting paid for it. They find themselves accepting dinner invitations, speaking engagements and so on that they would really like to refuse.

In restaurants the unassertive will never think of returning poorly cooked meals or complaining when they have been overcharged. In shops they will buy things that they don't really need or want because they are pressured to buy by a domineering salesman. In bus queues they'll find themselves being pushed out of the way by more self-important, assertive individuals.

Things reach a peak in hospital. There the unassertive patient will be put in bed, in pyjamas, and will stay there, confined and bound to conform. The unassertive patient will do what he is told to do, when he is told to do it. He will keep still and quiet and he won't ask questions.

Doctors and nurses like their patients to be unassertive because it makes the hospital easier to run. If all the patients keep still and don't ask too many questions, it makes life very easy for the nurses and the doctors. But the evidence shows that seriously ill patients who do not assert themselves are the patients who are the first to die. The patients who are considered 'model' patients and who are liked by the doctors and the nurses are the ones who don't survive.

The patients who survive are the assertive ones: the ones who demand information, who refuse to be dominated, who write down things that they are told, who want to be put into a good position near a window or the television set, who won't accept administrative nonsense just because everyone else accepts it, who want to know the reason behind every test and procedure, and who, in short, stick up for themselves as individuals. They demand to be allowed out of bed. They demand to be allowed home. They aren't very much liked by the doctors or the nurses. But they get better quicker and they survive.

The hospital situation is a rather special one, of course. But

111

outside hospital the non-assertive individual can suffer in a number of ways. As well as being physically and mentally worn out from doing chores for other people, he will often suffer a great deal of frustration and hidden anger. These feelings can be intense and extremely destructive, producing a wide range of physical and mental problems. Headaches and stomach pains are just two common physical consequences of an individual's failure to assert himself.

In fact, however, it is remarkably easy to become assertive and to gain in mental and physical health. The first thing to remember is that you don't have to be aggressive, rude or unpleasant. You simply have to be more aware of your own needs and wishes and more prepared to stand your ground when you are being put under pressure by someone else.

Naturally you won't always get your own way. But by learning how to assert yourself more effectively you will help yourself to stay healthier. You will gain enormously from the greater self-respect that you have and from being far less likely to spend most of your time on things you dislike.

To begin with you must remember to be straightforward and honest as often as possible. If you don't want to do something, say so. If you try to offer people explanations or excuses, you'll probably end up trapping yourself and being manipulated into a corner.

So, for example, if you are invited to attend a meeting and you try to get out of the meeting by saying that you are busy that day, you'll be trapped if the date of the meeting is changed. Your excuses will have implied that it is only the date that is making it difficult for you to attend. If you try to get out of something by saying that you don't have any particular skills for that kind of work, you'll simply encourage praise and flattery that will push you into accepting an offer or invitation that you'd have preferred to turn down.

You should be careful not to try and solve people's problems for them when they're trying to involve you in something you are anxious to avoid. If, for example, someone telephones you and asks you to speak to a group of people that you'd rather avoid, you'll end up trapping yourself if you start suggesting alternative speakers. The chances are that the people you suggest will either be unavailable or unsuitable. And when you can no longer help with useful alternatives you will find yourself accepting.

You can also help yourself by trying to put yourself into the position of an outside observer. Many people who are unassertive fail to look after themselves effectively because they are frightened of how they will appear to other people. But if you do put yourself in someone else's shoes, you'll often find that your behaviour really isn't as terrible as you first thought it was. Would you really think any the less of your best friend if she didn't invite her troublesome relatives to dinner every fortnight? Would you despise your best friend if she told her boss that she wasn't going to work on Sunday morning every week? Would you be horrified by the thought of someone sending back a poorly cooked meal in a restaurant or refusing to tip a surly and uncooperative waiter?

Once you start standing up for yourself a little, you'll soon find that you feel less frustrated. You'll feel more comfortable with other people too. And, most surprisingly perhaps, you'll find that other people treat you with respect and consideration.

Loving and caring

Researchers around the world have produced evidence to show that people of all ages can benefit from sharing a warm, caring relationship. Insurance companies in America, for example, have found that if a wife kisses her husband goodbye when he goes off to work every morning, he will be less likely to have car accidents on the way to the office or the factory. He will, on average, live five years longer than if she doesn't give him a morning kiss.

Babies are particularly likely to benefit from a close relationship with their mothers. They are especially likely to suffer if deprived of a close relationship. Evidence has been produced which shows that babies deprived of a close relationship with their mothers become emotionally unstable and develop more slowly than other babies.

There is, it seems, even a natural mechanism designed to help ensure that mothers and babies kiss one another as much as possible. During the last three months of pregnancy, and for the twelve months after a pregnancy has ended, a mother's lips

113

will produce sexually attractive chemicals designed to make her lips more kissable. Sebaceous glands along the borders of the newborn baby's lips produce similar chemicals and help ensure that the baby responds to its mother's kisses in an appropriate way.

As we grow up our need for a close, loving relationship with those who are nearest and dearest to us does not diminish. Children who are neglected by their parents, and deprived of a normal relationship with their parents as they grow up, will become 'harder' and 'tougher' in both physical and emotional terms. They will respond more slowly to signs of physical distress or pain and they will themselves show less affection to those around them.

Even in adulthood our need for love, care and affection does not fall. The healing power of a cuddle has, indeed, been so well established that in 1985 it was announced that double beds would be provided in the maternity units of some hospitals in Lincolnshire, so that husbands could cuddle and comfort their wives. In other hospitals doctors and nurses will often now turn a blind eye to patients in private rooms who want to turn visiting hours into personalized therapeutic experiences. Without these physical signs of affection we become more brittle, less emotionally stable and more susceptible to fear, stress, pressure and distress.

There are a number of simple ways in which you can increase the amount of loving in your life.

1   Try not to hide your feelings for those who are close to you. Don't be afraid to tell someone if you love them. Don't be shy about offering a kiss or a cuddle. And remember that it is just as important that you do not shy away when someone who is close to you approaches with a kiss, a hug or some other sign of physical affection.

2   Try to get rid of old-fashioned prejudices about showing affection in public. Members of previous generations often thought that it was wrong for courting couples to hold hands, for young mothers to breastfeed their babies in public or for couples to exchange kisses in the street.

These prejudices were based on nothing more substantial than an unhealthy mixture of religious guilt and unnatural embarrassment. There is nothing unnatural about sex, courtship or love. A few decades ago some people thought that nakedness was a sin and sex a duty to be endured by those prepared to procreate for the sake of society. Those attitudes are outdated and the time has come for the prejudices that they inspired to be discarded too. Learn to accept that there is nothing intrinsically wrong with two people hugging, kissing or cuddling in public. Until you have eradicated these fears and anxieties about public displays of affection, you will continue to find it difficult to enjoy or initiate private displays of affection.

3   Don't be shy about touching people – or allowing people to touch you. You may be able to break down some of your own barriers by having – or giving – a massage.

The word 'massage' has acquired a rather seedy reputation in recent years, thanks largely to the fact that it is frequently linked with such words as 'topless' and 'relief'. But a thorough massage can be extremely relaxing and soothing. It can help give us an excuse to touch one another. And it certainly can be therapeutic.

At one end of the spectrum it is sometimes possible to soothe a troubled individual to sleep by gently massaging his forearm with a single finger. As a junior hospital doctor I often used this technique with remarkable success when nursing elderly patients or small babies who couldn't get to sleep. It worked best with people at either end of the age spectrum – probably because they were least likely to feel embarrassed or shocked.

Alternatively, and more dramatically, a thorough kneading of the neck muscles can frequently help get rid of headaches and back pains. Neither of these are difficult skills to acquire, requiring nothing more than a couple of hands, some practice and a little lubrication to overcome natural friction. No one with a good friend needs ever pay for a decent massage.

When having – or giving – a massage it is also well worth remembering that a pleasant-smelling oil can help. In the first place, oils of any kind reduce the amount of friction between the skin of the person giving the massage and the skin of the individual receiving it. Second, they are of positive benefit because we all tend to respond well to good, therapeutic smells.

Olfactory influences are extremely effective at triggering off memories. In 1938, in a test conducted with a thousand women, it was shown that when one pair of stockings out of four was faintly perfumed, 96 per cent of all the women tested thought that those stockings were the best of the bunch – even though all the stockings were, in fact, made of exactly the same material.

More recently George Dodd and other research workers at Warwick University in England have conducted experiments with people under stress. They have shown that when individuals are given stressful tasks to do and, at the same time are exposed to an unfamiliar odour, they learn to associate the smell with the task. Then, when they are later exposed to the smell alone, they react to it as if they were under stress.

It is this simple relationship between smells and experiences which explains why hospital smells strike fear into otherwise brave individuals and why certain perfumes bring some men out in a sweat. It is the same sort of relationship which explains why some people become euphoric at the smell of freshly mown grass, while others tend to drool over the smell of hot tar. And it is the same relationship which explains why a relaxing massage with a pleasant smelling oil may be particularly beneficial.

4   Remember that children are particularly susceptible to a lack of affection. Newborn babies should be placed on their mother's stomachs as soon as possible after birth. And for the first few years of life babies need to be touched as often as possible by the people who are closest to them. In our society it is all too easy for a baby to spend its days in a pram or cot well away from people. That can be a destructive experience. Parents should try to keep their babies as close to them as they possibly can.

And remember that when a child starts to pay an unusual amount of attention to a doll (such as a teddy bear, for example), that child is crying out for more parental affection and love. There is a danger that the child who constantly needs to hug his teddy bear isn't getting enough affection from his parents.

Understanding your priorities

A few years ago a friend of mine decided that there was money to be made in the computer business. He didn't really know anything about computers, but he'd seen the queues of youngsters standing around in amusement arcades and public houses where there were computer games to be played. He made a few enquiries and found out that several companies were planning to start selling home computers. Within a few months he had taken a crash course in computer programming, borrowed a few thousand pounds from his bank manager and started a small company dedicated to the manufacture and sale of software designed to enable young computer users to play arcade games in their own homes.

The business proved to be far more successful than he had ever dared to hope. Within six months of marketing his first cassette he had to hire two dozen people to help him deal with the demand. The total turnover in his first twelve months exceeded a quarter of a million pounds. My friend was naturally delighted by the success of his venture. But he had tremendous difficulty in learning how to delegate authority and responsibility to the people working for him. He had hired an accountant, but he still insisted on signing every cheque and examining every invoice. He had several programmers working for him, but he still tried to check through all the work they did. He had an experienced production manager working for him, but still he insisted on keeping a close eye on production.

He became obsessed with the minutiae of his business and spent most of his time checking figures and cassette labels and examining new programs. He arrived at work at seven thirty every morning and didn't leave until ten at night. He worked on Sundays, Saturdays and Bank Holidays. He gave everything to his business. He developed a stomach ulcer and started getting regular migraines. He gave his time, his energy and his health.

Two years after setting up the company he looked likely to become a millionaire. A year after that he was bankrupt. While he had been spending his time dealing with the small, day-to-day problems of his business, he had entirely failed to notice that the market was changing. He had neither the time nor the energy to see the need to diversify. When the demand for games programs for home computer machines disappeared almost overnight his business collapsed. Because he had been obsessed with minor problems he had been unable to spot the warning signs which should have told him that he needed to introduce new ideas and new concepts to his company.

My friend isn't the only person to have failed to see things in proper perspective. Ex-President Lyndon B. Johnson is said to have spent a good deal of time helping to redesign Air Force uniform trousers. And Jimmy Carter is said to have insisted on arranging the tennis schedule for the White House tennis court, even when he should have been thinking about much larger and more important problems.

This type of failure to differentiate between those important problems which need a considerable amount of attention, and the far less significant problems which can be safely delegated, ignored or simply left to other people, doesn't just lead to economic or political disaster, of course. It can lead to a wide variety of health problems. Pressures, worries and problems of all sizes can have an adverse effect on your body and your mind and the smaller problems and the insignificant worries can have just as devastating an effect on your health as the major problems.

If you fail to differentiate between the big problems and the little ones, and you fail to establish priorities in your life, you will suffer in a number of ways. First, the number of problems you're exposed to will prove damaging simply because there are so many of them. If you allow yourself to worry about the scratch on your car and the missing button on your shirt sleeve, your mind will simply add these anxieties to the other more essential worries that you have. Unless you make a conscious decision to separate minor problems from major problems your mind will treat them all in the same way.

Second, while you are spending valuable time worrying about minor difficulties, you will fail to solve the major problems which need your attention. While my friend was worrying about what colour boxes his computer cassettes should be packed in the market's requirements were changing. While you're worrying about your missing shirt button you may fail to spot the business opportunity of a lifetime. And while you make yourself ill worrying about minor problems the major difficulties will be getting worse and worse – with the result that in the end you'll have even greater problems.

Finally, your failure to establish genuine priorities in your life will mean that you spend too much of your time on the things which really don't matter and too little time on the things which do matter. The businessman who spends every waking hour making money so that his family can have all the things that money can buy, may well wake up one morning to the realization that he doesn't 'know' his wife and that his children have grown up as strangers. Learning how to differentiate between the trivia and the essentials in your life is an important part of staying alive and healthy.

Getting your priorities sorted out really isn't all that difficult. But it will take a little time. The following list of suggestions should help you.

1   It may sound exceptionally simplistic, but the first thing you have to do is to decide exactly what is important to you. That may sound easier than it is. But before you can decide which things are unimportant to you, you must know what your priorities are. You must decide exactly what you want to do with your life. Is your family more important than your work? Or must your career take precedence over everything else? Is your hobby more important than your work? What would you do – and not do – to further your ambitions? What limits are there? Is having time to sit and relax and enjoy life more important than becoming rich and successful? Are your children more important than anything else? Is a wonderful home in a pleasant part of the country your main aim?

You must also decide just how important money is to you. What are your material needs? How far is your life being controlled by the material needs of others? If other people's material needs are dominating your life, you must decide just how important the needs – and the individuals – are to you. Are the sacrifices you have to make acceptable? How far are your needs being influenced by what you think other people want (as opposed to what they really want)? And how can you best adapt your life to suit your needs?

When making out the list of things that are important to you, don't forget to include the simpler things in life. We tend to think of homes, cars and material possessions as being the most important things in our lives. They may well be. But there are many pleasures available which won't cost you a penny to enjoy. Lying on your back watching the clouds float by, having a cat sit on your lap, spending a warm day on the beach, walking in the rain, sitting by an old-fashioned log fire toasting muffins – many of the most enjoyable things in life won't cost you much at all.

But if you are going to enjoy these things, you will have to be prepared to make some special effort and leave a little time free from everyday hassles. Work out how many of the important things in your life you need money for. And work out how many need people. Work out too how many of the things you really enjoy are missing from your world because of your current lifestyle. If your priorities have been determined by other people, you may well spend a large proportion of your time on striving for success that you don't really need or want, while at the same time missing out on the things which should really give you pleasure.

Remember to include your health in your list of priorities. How important is your health? And are you giving your health the attention it warrants?

2 Make a list of all the things in your life that are causing you stress. Then look through your list and try to decide what you can do about the problems which are causing you the greatest amount of worry. You may be able to delegate some problems to others. You may be able to deal with worries by taking specific action. You may be able to find help or share tasks with other people.

By deciding what your priorities are you should be able to concentrate on the problems which are most important to you and dismiss, shelve or deal with the less important problems.

While sorting through your problems, remember that it isn't stress that causes the difficulties so much as your response and reaction to stress.

3 Learn to say 'no' to people when they want you to do things which are likely to eat into your time or disrupt your personal list of priorities. If you are constantly doing things that strangers want you to do, the chances are that the people who really matter will suffer. Don't hesitate to refuse to take on tasks that are not particularly important to you or those who matter in your life.

Remember, too that no one is indispensable. If you wander into a cemetery, you'll be surrounded by people who all thought that the world depended on their doing this or that in a hurry. Your saying 'no' occasionally isn't going to stop the world going round.

4   When you are faced with a problem, try to see it in perspective. Is a bad golf shot really likely to ruin your whole life? Is a missing sock going to disrupt your whole week? Is your career so delicately balanced that a missing train will result in your financial ruin? Is a leaky washing machine going to stop you ever having any fun in life?

5   Try to plan your life a little and put your ambitions, aims and priorities in some sort of perspective. What do you want to be doing in five, ten and fifteen years' time? How many of the things that you worry about every day would you spend your time on if this was your last day on earth? And how important will some of today's major problems seem in five years' – or even six months' – time?

Then decide how best you can achieve your aims, and tackle your problems one by one. When Horatius was defending his Roman bridge against the invading Etruscan army, he tackled each opponent one at a time. If he'd worried about how he was going to deal with the rest of the force that was facing him, he would have never got anywhere. But by being realistic and taking his problems one at a time he was far more successful than he could have dared imagine.

6   Don't let yourself be fooled into spending time, effort and energy on products or ambitions that are not important to you. If you buy a cottage in the country so that your friends, neighbours and relatives will know that you are successful and rich, you'll gain very little from the purchase if you then have to spend every weekend cleaning out the gutters, retiling the roof, repairing the fences and coping with the overgrown garden. If you buy a fancy Italian car to impress strangers on the motorway, you'll pay a higher price when you have to fork out a king's ransom to insure it and a fortune to get it serviced. If you have a swimming pool put into your garden and spend most of the summer fishing out the leaves, the slugs and the neighbours' noisy children, you'll probably wish you'd been less anxious to impress everyone.

You'll be able to protect yourself against stresses of this sort only by sorting out your priorities beforehand.

7   Don't ever make unrealistic goals for yourself. If you do, you'll end up suffering from stress and anxiety produced by frustration. When you've decided on your priorities and

you're planning on changing your life, keep your immediate ambitions small and within reach. That way you'll get accustomed to success. If, for example, you want to lose fifty pounds of excess weight, don't start off with such a massive goal; instead plan on getting rid of, say, ten pounds in your first full month of dieting. At the end of that month aim at another ten pounds' loss in another month.

CHAPTER 7

Mindpower techniques

Tranquillity

Roger (not his real name, of course) is a good friend of mine who has worked as a television presenter for several years. During that time he has expended a considerable amount of energy fighting a worrying assortment of stress-induced problems. Early in his career he developed a stomach ulcer and that was soon followed by a raised blood pressure. He has also suffered from persistent arthritis in his knees. To help him to confront the day-to-day pressures of presenting a live television programme he has regularly used cigarettes and tranquillizing drugs.

Inevitably, all these problems began to have an adverse effect on his skills as a performer. His edginess began to show through on the programme and the drugs he needed to help him stay reasonably calm began to affect his ability to think quickly when things went wrong. One of the producers working on the programme told him that they were thinking of terminating his contract and suggested that if he found work in front of the camera too nerve-racking, he would perhaps be well advised to look for a job behind the scenes.

This warning was a blessing in disguise, for although it frightened Roger and meant that for a week or two he needed even larger amounts of tranquillizers, it inspired him to try and do something positive about his problem.

When I first suggested 'daydreaming' as a permanent solution, Roger was sceptical. He thought it sounded rather silly and far too simplistic to work for him. But he was desperate and knew that he had to try something if he was to retain both his sanity and his job. So he decided to try it.

When things were getting particularly hectic during the hours before a programme was due to start, Roger learnt to disappear for ten minutes and go and sit in his dressing room. He would lock the door and stuff some cotton wool into his ears to cut out the noise from outside. Then he would settle back in a comfortable chair, close his eyes and imagine that he was sunning himself on a beach somewhere. He would position his chair so that it was underneath the room's most powerful lamp and, with his eyes closed, he would imagine that the heat he could feel from the lamp was being produced by the sun's rays. After ten minutes of mental relaxation he would emerge from his dressing room refreshed and ready to carry on preparing for the show.

After a couple of weeks he found that he didn't even need to lock himself in his dressing room in order to 'escape' from all the pressures that were surrounding him. He needed only to close his eyes and find somewhere comfortable to sit for a few moments. He found that he could even manage to relax in the studio, imagining that the heat from the strong studio lights was summer sunlight. His mind would do the rest.

Roger now manages to cope with the stresses in his life quite effectively. He no longer has high blood pressure or indigestion and he doesn't need to take tranquillizers. He hasn't given up smoking completely, but he has cut down. Most important of all as far as he is concerned, his calmness and sense of tranquillity have improved his performance and removed the producer's doubts about his suitability for the job.

I could quote dozens of other case histories to prove exactly the same point. And so could many others working in this same field of medicine. There is convincing scientific evidence now to show that any individual who learns how to deal with stress by relaxing his mind will benefit in a variety of different ways. He will be stronger, healthier and far less vulnerable to worry and anxiety than the individual who is at the mercy of each day's new stresses and strains.

Under normal circumstances an almost unending stream of facts and feelings will pour into your mind. Your eyes and your ears will join with your other senses in gathering an enormous variety of bits and pieces of information. Each one of those pieces will itself produce assessments, interpretations and conclusions. Even when you aren't consciously thinking of anything, or putting yourself under pressure, thousands of sensory messages will keep your body busy adapting to changes in your environment.

If you can cut down the amount of information that your mind is receiving, you will cut down the number of mental responses that take place. You will become rested and relaxed and your body and your mind will benefit in a number of positive ways. If you suffer from any stress-induced disorders (such as high blood pressure, colitis, asthma, indigestion or eczema, for example), you will benefit enormously. If you suffer from any stress-induced mental problems (such as anxiety or insomnia, for example), that problem also will diminish in importance. And you will benefit by feeling stronger and healthier and by being more resistant to disease and disorder of every kind.

Many of us find it difficult to reduce the amount of information pouring into our minds because we feel guilty if we slow down. We feel that we are failing ourselves and those around us if we sit and watch the world go by for a minute or two. We've been conditioned to think that only by pushing ourselves as hard as possible will we ever achieve anything worthwhile or win the respect of those around us.

Pressured by expectations, we are always in a hurry, rushing from crisis to crisis and struggling to cram as much as we possibly can into every moment of our lives. We rush through life at top speed, making ourselves ill by pushing ourselves so hard, and failing to gain any real pleasure from the things we do because we are doing them so quickly. We hurtle along beautiful country roads at breakneck pace, seeing little of the world and gaining little from our constant hurrying.

Of course, it isn't always easy to know exactly how to set about doing nothing. If you sit in the garden, you'll probably be disturbed by the noises of your neighbour's lawn mower. Or you'll spot weeds that need to be pulled. Or someone will come round and interrupt your reverie. But there are ways of doing nothing in such a way that people will leave you alone.

You could try taking up a hobby such as fishing that involves a lot of sitting still and very little else. It's an excellent way to relax your mind. Or become an avid spectator of a peaceful sport such as cricket or bowls. Settle down in your local park and watch a match and people will usually leave you alone as long as you like.

Or find a comfortable bench by the seaside. I know of few things as relaxing as watching a gentle sea breaking on a sandy shore or pebbly beach. It is almost impossible to stay irritated or anxious when you're watching the sea. If you can't find a bench where you aren't likely to be disturbed by noisy children or people hungry for conversation, then simply take your own deckchair or find a lonely rock. Alternatively, seek out a café where you can sit for as long as you like with a single cup of coffee or a glass of lemon tea. And just sit and stare and watch the people go by. Parisian and Viennese cafés are excellent for doing nothing.

Try taking the telephone off the hook and run yourself a warm bath. A shower may be the most hygienic way to wash yourself, but nothing is quite as relaxing as a warm bath. Make sure that there is plenty of fresh hot water available so that you can keep the temperature at a comfortable level. And then just lie back and enjoy the warmth and the peace. It's as close as you or I will ever get to being back in the womb.

Or try lying down in a country field, or even a church graveyard. (There are few places as peaceful and relaxing as graveyards.) And then just watch the clouds wandering by overhead. If it's raining, find a quiet church and spend ten or fifteen minutes in peaceful contemplation. You don't have to be a member of any official religious group to enjoy the peace available there.

As a final resort, if you've been under pressure and you feel stressed and strained, try to take a couple of days away from it all. Don't hurry away and try to visit six different countries or rush off in an attempt to drive half way across Europe, or try to break the world waterspeed record. Plan on spending a couple of days in a peaceful country hotel that is miles from anywhere and where you can linger over breakfast, sit around doing very little and pamper yourself a good deal. If you can't go away for any reason, have a relaxing time at home. Don't listen to the radio or watch television (use music cassettes and film videos for entertainment). Take the telephone off the hook. Avoid any chores. And tell any potential visitors that you're going 'away' for the weekend. Get in a supply of entertaining books

126

and magazines.

You'll benefit enormously by allowing your mind to rest and roam free in this sort of way. You may even find that stored-up ideas and worries drift into sight. Keep a notebook by your side and jot them down as they come into view. If, when you try to relax by doing nothing, you find that your mind fills up completely and uncomfortably with worries, thoughts and anxieties (worries you can't get rid of by simply writing them down) you need to cut the flow of potentially harmful data pouring into your brain. You need to learn how to daydream.

Most of us daydream when we are small. But our teachers and our parents teach us that it is a wasteful, undesirable habit that we must lose. In fact, it isn't a bad habit at all. It is, on the contrary, a natural technique which can help you relax your mind thoroughly and achieve a beneficial level of tranquillity even when things around you are just as hectic as ever. (Few places are as hectic as a television studio and yet my friend Roger manages to daydream very effectively.) When you daydream, you use a cut-out process which your mind has available but which it has forgotton how to use.

To daydream effectively you have to allow your imagination to dominate your thinking and to take over your body too. It really isn't a difficult trick to master and once you've learned how to do it, you'll be able to use the technique wherever you happen to be and whatever you happen to be doing. (Although I must warn you that the daydreaming technique is so effective that you should not try it while driving or operating machinery of any kind.)

To begin with, you have to learn how to practise. Learning to daydream is a bit like learning to play golf or learning how to dance. If you don't practise it will never come easily or naturally.

Start by finding somewhere comfortable to lie down. Your bedroom is probably the best place. Close the door and lock it if you can. Put a 'Do Not Disturb' notice on the outside door handle. Before you go into your room, by the way, take the telephone off the hook, put the cats out and make sure that there isn't anyone due to call or arrive home for fifteen or twenty minutes or so.

Now, lie down on your bed and make yourself as comfort-able as you can get. Take big, deep breaths and try to conjure up some particularly restful and relaxing scene from your past. Don't let anyone else wander into your daydream because if you do the chances are that your daydream will either become a fantasy or a nightmare.

You can, of course, use just about any scene you like when you are daydreaming. And you can even build up a library of your very own private daydreams as the months go by. You can store a valuable personal collection of happy memories – some of them can be real, some may be memories taken from films or television programmes, others may be based on scenes that you've encountered in favourite books or magazine stories.

To give you an idea of the sort of daydream that will prove most effective I have prepared three simple ones. Either read through these scenes and learn them by heart, or ask someone close to you to read these words out slowly and softly while you are lying down and feeling as relaxed and comfortable as possible.

DAYDREAM ONE

Imagine that you are in a dressing gown lying down on a large, soft, four-poster bed in a country hotel. Above your head the bed is hung with a brocade canopy made of a rich red and gold material. Matching curtains hang at all four corners of the bed and are tied back with red ropes, knotted neatly into bows. The room is panelled in oak and there is one window on your right. It is an old-fashioned metal lattice-work window with thick, red, velvet curtains hanging on each side of it. Through the window you can see a corner of a peaceful, typically English country garden and beyond, in the distance, there are pleasant acres of rolling countryside. In front of the window there is a long window seat covered in material that matches the curtains.

To your left as you lie on the bed there is a door. This is almost impossible to distinguish from the walls, being made from exactly the same sort of panelled oak. A large key protrudes from the lock and a bolt has been drawn as an added security.

You don't know what the weather is like outside, but in your bedroom it is warm and cosy. Directly in front of your bed there is a large open fireplace and a wood fire is crackling

128

away. The fire itself looks solid enough to last for several hours, but there is a huge pile of fresh logs stacked neatly in the hearth.

Your eyes are closed as you lie back on your bed, but you can hear the crackle of the fire and feel its warmth. Outside you can hear the birds and a few farmyard animals in the far distance. A gentle breeze plays with the tops of the nearby trees. There is a faint smell of woodsmoke in the room.

You lie back, drifting comfortably into a sleepy sort of state and knowing that you have nothing to do for several hours. You've had a fairly tiring morning walking through the countryside and your damp outdoor clothes are all being dried downstairs. You've had lunch and had a bath and have several hours to go before dinner. The hotel staff who are looking after you are quiet, caring and considerate. They obviously feel well-disposed towards you and you know that your evening is going to be peaceful and enjoyable. You have nothing to do but rest, doze and drift peacefully and calmly into a sleepy and relaxing state of mind.

DAYDREAM TWO

Imagine that you are lying on a warm, sunny beach. It is a mid-summer day and yet the beach is quite deserted. In the distance to your right and to your left there are one or two families scattered around and you can hear the faint sound of children playing. In front of you the waves are breaking gently on the soft sand and behind you a slight breeze rustles through the long grasses growing in the sand dunes. High above, you can hear seagulls calling to one another as they circle overhead. They and the far-off children are the only sounds that disturb the peace and tranquillity of the afternoon.

The most insistent sensation is, however, that of warmth. The sand underneath you is warm and the sun is warm on your skin. You've oiled yourself carefully with sun lotion and you can smell it still. If you opened your eyes, you'd be able to see your skin glistening in the sunshine. But the sun is bright on your eyelids and you don't want to open your eyes just yet. Still and peaceful, you soak up the sun and enjoy the afternoon warmth. (If you find it difficult to create this scene, try using a sunlamp to simulate the warmth of the sun and a sound effects record to create the sound of the sea.)

DAYDREAM THREE

Imagine that you are lying back on a grassy bank by the side of a slow-moving stream. It is a clear, fresh stream with the pebbles that make up its base clearly visible through the bright water. As the stream meanders along, you can hear the sound it makes rippling over the pebbles. You can hear birds up above you in the branches of a huge oak tree. You can hear insects in the fields behind you and in the field across the stream you can hear the occasional sheep. High in the sky there are birds circling, but you cannot see them for the sun is too bright for you to open your eyes. It is a warm, relaxing summer sun and the gentle coolness of the grassy bank on which you lie makes a pleasant contrast.

If you find it difficult to recreate one of these images, hunt out an old photograph or postcard of some spot that you remember as restful, peaceful and relaxing. Carry the photograph with you and look at it through half-closed eyes as often as you can. Try to imagine yourself there once again. Try to remember all the relevant sensations: the sounds, the smells, the temperature and so on. Try to see yourself in that relaxing situation as often as you possibly can.

In future when you go on holiday collect postcards of the places that you find comfortable and calming. Take your own photographs too and if possible get someone to take photographs showing you sitting or lying somewhere peaceful, comfortable and relaxing. Then carry these postcards and photographs around with you.

Daydreaming has one important advantage over the type of meditation favoured by some doctors and many religious groups. With meditation you have to empty your mind completely and replace real anxieties and troubles with a clinically empty, clean space. That isn't easy to do. When you daydream, you replace your natural fears with calming, comfortable, tranquil memories which do themselves have a useful and positive effect. Meditation does undoubtedly halt the damage caused by the pressures of the outside world. But when you fill the void instead with peaceful, tranquil thoughts, you don't just halt the damage – you do much more. You can build up your inner strength by filling your mind with positive, health-giving feelings. Once you have learned how to daydream properly then you will be able to use the same technique just about wherever you are and whatever you are doing. If you're stuck in a traffic jam, for example, and you feel your heart rate rising and your muscles tensing, just lie back and get as comfortable as you can. Close your eyes and imagine that you are on your beach or in your country hotel. Replace the real fears and frustrations of the world around you with the relaxing feelings and memories of a scene that you find soothing and calming.

Similarly, you can try the same technique when you are sitting in an office and besieged by people anxious for your attention. Take a few minutes off and rest completely and properly. If there is nowhere else to do your daydreaming, disappear into the washroom. A few minutes' relaxation will help you work far more effectively and efficiently.

Incidentally, if you do want to prove to yourself just how useful this technique can be, take your pulse when you start a daydreaming session and then take your pulse again when you finish. You'll almost certainly find that your pulse rate will fall noticeably during a ten- or fifteen-minute daydreaming session.

Try not to make this a routine test, however. It is all too easy to turn a relaxation technique into a competitive exercise. You won't benefit from this technique if you end up trying to get your pulse rate lower and lower or worrying about the natural variations in your heart rate.

Finally, a word of warning. When you have relaxed don't get up suddenly. If you have relaxed efficiently, your blood pressure will have fallen fairly considerably. And if you do get up too quickly, you'll probably feel rather dizzy. Instead, stretch your arms and legs carefully and gently for a minute or two. If you've been lying down move slowly into a sitting position and stay like that for a few seconds more in order to give your body time to re-adapt.

Physical relaxation

Your mind has a number of very obvious effects on your body. If you get angry, your skin will go red. If you are afraid, your skin will go pale and you may sweat. Your heart will beat faster and your muscles will tense. Your rate of breathing may increase and, if you are susceptible to asthma, you'll probably start to wheeze as well.

All these changes can produce a number of quite devastating physical effects. For example, tensed muscles commonly produce headaches, back pains and stiff necks. If you suffer from any problem caused by physical tension, all sorts of professionals will be able to help you. Orthodox doctors can help you deal with the symptoms of disease. And if your symptoms are produced by muscle tension, a physiotherapist or masseur should be able to help you by relaxing your muscles.

But by seeking help from a medical professional when you are suffering from a stress-induced disorder, can only provide you with a short-term solution. It's obviously much more sensible to learn how to deal with your symptoms yourself. The ancient Chinese used to point out that if you give a man a fish you feed him for a day, whereas if you teach him how to fish you feed him for a lifetime. And the same is true of relaxation.

If a professional helps to relax a patient's tensed muscles, he'll provide an immediate solution. If, however, the patient can learn how to relax his own muscles – and how to keep his muscles relaxed when he is in stressful situations – he'll have access to a permanent solution that can be used at any time.

It isn't difficult to learn how to help your mind by relaxing your body. Select one of the following techniques.

1   Take slow, deep breaths. Anger or fear will make you breathe faster. You can, however, soothe your mind by deliberately taking slower, deeper breaths. If you are anxious because you are about to make a public speech, try taking long, slow, deep breaths. You'll find that your anxiety will be kept under control.

2   Keep your voice as low as you can. Anger and other emotions often make you want to shout. Sometimes you must let your anger out. But if that is totally inappropriate, whisper – and you'll find it difficult to stay angry.

3   Learn to relax your muscles. When you are angry or upset, your muscles will become tense. That tension will then produce symptoms such as muscle pains and headaches. You can deal with those symptoms and help reduce the tension in

your mind by deliberately relaxing your body.

Next time you are so angry that your muscles are tense and your fists clenched, try lying down and deliberately loosening and relaxing all your muscles. You'll probably find that your anger just fades away. It is remarkably difficult to stay angry when you are completely relaxed.

To learn how to relax all your muscles begin by clenching the muscles of your left hand as firmly as you possibly can. Make a fist as though you were about to punch someone. Your knuckles will eventually turn white and your hand will become quite painful. If you now let your fist unfold, you will feel the muscle relax. To relax your body completely use this same technique to tense and relax all your muscles group by group. Within fifteen minutes or so you should have managed to relax every group of muscles in your body.

4   Remember that tiring physical work can be extremely relaxing. Do not overdo things, of course. You must stop as soon as your muscles begin to ache. But chopping wood or digging the garden can be extremely therapeutic. It is possible to ease a troubled mind by simple physical exertion. If you are not fit enough to chop wood or you have no garden to dig, I recommend a good, brisk walk. It is an excellent way to get rid of muscle tension.

5   Muscles which are tense and sore can be eased by simple massage – and the soothing effect that the massage has on the muscles will also soothe the mind. (The link between mind and body is a close one: a tense mind can produce tense muscles, and soothed, relaxed muscles can also produce a soothed, relaxed mind.) You can massage your own feet, legs and arms and may even be able to massage your own neck muscles. But back problems are best massaged by another pair of hands. Remember that a little oil will make massage far more soothing and effective as a restorative (*See* also pages 115–16).

Mental imagery

The relationship between imagination and reality is closer than you think. And it is a relationship that has been acknowledged and accepted for a long time. William

Shakespeare wrote that, 'there is nothing good or bad, but thinking makes it so.' And more recently the philosopher William James announced that in his opinion, too, human beings could, by changing the inner attitudes of their minds, change the outer aspects of their lives, and thereby control their own destinies.

Only in the last few years, however, have these philosophical conclusions been translated into practical reality. While the majority of physicians and surgeons around the world have continued to concentrate on using knives, poisons, electricity, chemicals and radiation to attack disease and disorder (forgetting that the battleground, the human body, is often as vulnerable to the weapons being employed as the disease itself), a small but persistent number of researchers has continued to experiment with techniques involving the imagination. It is a weapon that is both simple and sophisticated, commonplace and unique, remarkably easy to use and yet far more powerful than any other available tool.

As is well known, the human imagination can prove destructive and damaging. If a man thinks he has a cancer developing, there is a very good chance indeed that he will develop a cancer. If a woman thinks she is going to lose her baby, the chances of her losing the baby are greatly enhanced. If a man thinks he is going to have a heart attack, he will probably have a heart attack. If a woman thinks she is likely to die, she will probably die.

It is this power of the imagination over the body that accounts for the strengths of the voodoo priest and the African witchdoctor. It is the same power that underpins the doctor's ability to convince his patients of his own infallibility. It is the same power that explains the placebo effect and the ability of an untrained healer to conquer pain and disease with nothing more mysterious than his own hands.

In the past the power of the imagination has been used almost exclusively as a method of augmenting the unnatural skills of the interventionist. The general practitioner and the hospital specialist use their patients' imaginations when telling them that the prescription they are providing will banish their symptoms. The homoeopath, the hypnotherapist, the acupuncturist and the herbalist all use the imagination to augment and enhance their own limited technical skills. When the

134

professional suggests to the patient that he will get better, the patient's imagination responds by triggering the release of natural pain-relieving hormones (or endorphins). And when the patient duly gets better, the professional usually takes the credit.

Recently, however, it has become clear that in order to harness the power of his imagination the patient does not necessarily need the help of a medical professional. He needs only to believe in the power of his imagination in order to benefit from its potential strength. He has to learn a few simple creative 'tricks' in order to harness these powers, but the basic requirement, the fundamental, essential prerequisite is that he believes.

To walk a tightrope you need faith in your skills and you need to believe that you will succeed. If you do not have that faith and belief, however great your skills may be, you will fall. To use your imagination to help you fight illness and disease you need just that type of faith and belief in your own abilities. In order to build up your faith in your imagination I suggest that you start by practising the day-dreaming exercises described on pages 128–30. You don't need to spend long on the exercises – five or ten minutes will do – but practise them as often as you can. In addition to these general exercises, there are one or two other, more specific exercises that you can try.

First, cut a lemon in two and suck a little of the juice out of one half. Concentrate hard on the taste and the bitterness and try to be aware of all your reactions. Notice how your mouth fills with saliva, how your nose automatically wrinkles up in distaste and how you find yourself almost backing away from the lemon. A couple of hours later try to imagine that you are sucking that lemon again. Use your imagination to help you taste the bitterness and you'll soon notice your mouth becoming moist with saliva. You'll notice too that your nose automatically wrinkles again.

You can repeat this simple exercise as often as you like. It will help give you confidence in your ability to recreate scenes with the aid of your imagination. And as your mouth automatically waters every time, you'll have positive evidence to show that your imagination is working.

When you fall ill and need to use the powers of your imagination to help you combat very real symptoms, there are a number of simple ways in which you can stimulate your imagination to help you.

1 Always think of yourself getting better and try to see yourself fully recovered, doing all the things you would normally do. If you develop the early symptoms of a cold and you visualize yourself snuffling away in bed and missing all sorts of important appointments, you'll probably end up in bed with a terrible cold – missing all sorts of important appointments.

If, however, you see yourself recovering from your cold after a few hours mild snuffling, the cold symptoms will disappear and you won't need to miss any appointments at all. Naturally, I'm not promising that you can stay healthy all the time simply by seeing yourself as healthy – some genuine problems will require outside help – but minor troubles such as coughs, colds and aches and pains can often be defeated in this simple way. And even when your imagination on its own cannot defeat illness, it is much better to have it working on your side than to have it contributing strength to your illness. At the very worst, your imagination will help minimize the length of time that you are ill.

2 Never think of any disease as being strong or powerful. Always think of your body as being stronger than any attacking force. If you have an infection of any kind, think of the infective organisms as being evil, but weak, homeless, lonely and frightened. And think of your body as a tower of strength. If you have a cancer, think of it as an uncertain intruder, struggling to survive. If you think of a cancer or infection as a 'being', think of it as weak and weedy, having a hacking cough and terrible skin.

3 Try leaving your body if you are suffering from pain or some specific illness. Decide that you'll move to a far corner of the room and settle yourself down to help heal your body. Imagine that you can see yourself from the front, the side, the back and from above. Leave the pain or the illness behind. Now see teams of skilled and dedicated doctors working on your body to remove the disease and eradicate the pain. Visualize the disease as a pile of rubbish that simply needs to be cleaned out and carted away. Imagine that the pain in your

body is being transmitted along special wires and try to see the doctors cutting those wires. Don't re-enter your body until you are satisfied that the doctors have done as much as they can for the time being.

4   If you are being treated with drugs of any kind imagine each tablet or capsule as being full of special miniature fighting forces. Imagine those forces being released in your stomach, finding their way into your bloodstream and travelling around your body fighting the disease that is affecting you. Imagine the white blood cells in your body fighting also on your behalf. Think of your fighting forces as cowboys, as cavalry, as spacemen or as mediaeval knights of the Round Table. It really doesn't matter how you use your imagination as long as you use it in a positive and dramatic way and as long as you pick images in which you can believe in and have faith.

Some of this may sound alarmingly simple. But that is only because we have been trained to think of medical technology as having all the answers and of our bodies as being fundamentally weak and fragile. As children we are told off for fantasizing and daydreaming. As adults we are encouraged to put our faith in the professionals. And yet all the evidence now available shows that the professionals have very few answers, while our bodies contain many forces that we have consistently underestimated. Our minds can make our bodies ill. But they can also keep them healthy – and make them well again.

The healing touch

There is quite a difference between ordinary 'healing' and 'faith healing'. With faith healing (or spiritual healing), the healer needs to call on some supernatural force, some god or religious being, who will offer a cure; usually in return for some form of prayer, pilgrimage or supplication.

Many modern healers don't really approve of faith healing, however. And healing certainly isn't necessarily mystical, nor does it need to be associated with any religion or religious group. In the last few years healing has indeed become a thriving alternative medical speciality, quite divorced from religion. In Britain alone the Confederation of Healing

137

Organizations represents no less than nine separate healing groups and some seven thousand individual healers. Most surprising of all, perhaps, is the fact that the majority of practising healers do not believe that there is anything particularly exceptional in what they do. 'Healing', one healer has said, 'is not a special gift, it's just that the full-time healers practise a lot and get quite good at it.'

Over the years healers have been regarded with considerable scepticism by many people. And yet there is a considerable amount of evidence around to show that healing does have a useful effect on many patients. Back in the 1950s Bernard Grad, a biochemist working at McGill University in Montreal anaesthetized some mice, made small cuts in their skin and divided them into two groups. Group one were left to heal by themselves, without any treatment at all. The mice in group two were healed by a professional healer. And the mice in group two healed more quickly than the others.

Even more convincing (since her work has involved human patients) Dolores Krieger, Professor of Nursing at New York University and one of the best known healers in the world, has convinced many sceptical doctors by running controlled clinical trials which have shown that blood changes produced by healing can be measured in the laboratory. You really can't get better evidence than that.

Today a number of research programmes are studying the effects of healing on patients suffering from diseases such as rheumatoid arthritis, where it is possible to measure the levels of improvement quite specifically. Just what these research projects will show is still something of a mystery. But one thing that already seems clear is that despite Bernard Grad's experiment with mice, healers do seem to get better results when the subject knows that he or she is being healed and positively wants to get better. Healing, it seems, works by releasing the individual patient's own internal personal healing powers.

Indeed, a good many healers seem to agree that although there may be some benefit to be gained from visiting a professional healer, most people can use healing techniques themselves. Anyone, it seems, can become a healer. The only advantage of going to see a healing professional is that you benefit from his or her strength of personality and enthusiasm.

To use your own healing powers place your hands on or close to your patient's body. And then simply project a feeling of well-being, comfort and good health from your body to theirs.

If you want to check your own healing potential, there is a simple experiment that you can try. Start by putting your hands close together, with your fingers pointing away from you as though you were praying. Don't quite let your hands touch, but get them as close together as you possibly can. Now separate your hands by two inches and keep them apart for a few seconds. Then return them to your original position – with your hands close together without actually touching. Keep your hands in that position for a few more seconds and then separate them by four inches. Once again keep them apart for a few seconds.

After returning your hands back to your original position, separate them by six inches. Do this as slowly as you possibly can and remember to stay in each different position for a few seconds at a time. Finally, separate your hands by eight or ten inches and then slowly bring them back together again in rather jerky, two-inch movements. You may well feel a strange sort of bounciness, as though the air were being compressed between your hands, but you'll probably also notice a change in the skin temperature of your hands. They may become a little warmer or simply tingle, but with most people the changes make the skin slightly cooler.

Intuition

A decade or two ago you would have had difficulty in finding any reputable scientist prepared to admit that he believed in telepathy or extra sensory perception. These days you'd have just as much difficulty in finding a reputable scientist prepared to say categorically that he did not believe in parapsychology. In America the Federal Bureau of Investigation has hired psychics to help them solve crimes; the Pentagon has invested millions in the whole subject of parapsychology. Around the world many intelligent and well-placed individuals have sought personal and professional advice from people with undefined powers of this kind.

As the whole subject becomes better known, so too

increasing numbers of people provide us with practical illustrations of the remarkable ways in which the mind often operates. There have been countless stories of individuals having dreams and then discovering that their dreams were very close to reality. The mind, it seems, can work in many remarkable ways.

One continuing problem is that is only too easy to pick out specific instances and examples of intuition and exaggerate or distort their importance. But even allowing for this, there is little doubt that most of us do have skills that we use only too rarely. Nor is there any doubt that by taking greater advantage of these skills we could deal with many of our daily problems far more readily, and with far less stress and heartache.

If you want to use your intuitive powers more constructively, read through the following paragraphs.

1   If you tend to spend ages making relatively minor decisions – and find yourself getting into quite a state trying to decide what to wear, what to eat and so on – then give yourself a ten-second limit for making your decision. You'll find this a remarkably liberating exercise. Simply make your mind up to follow whatever thought sprang first into your mind. If your first instinct was to put on your red dress or blue suit, do just that. Don't waste mental energy thinking about it for an hour and trying on everything in your wardrobe. Similarly, if your first instinct tells you to order the steak, order it. Don't spend half an hour worrying about whether to order the steak or the lamb cutlets. The chances are that your first, instinctive solution was probably the best. And with fairly minor decisions like these you haven't got much to lose anyway. The longer you spend worrying before coming to a conclusion, the greater the price you'll have to pay for defying your sense of intuition.

Remember too that if you don't do what your instinct tells you to do, you'll curse yourself afterwards, and probably never be really satisfied with your solution.

2   If you have a difficult problem to solve and you've spent hours worrying about it, give up and do something completely different. Take a walk or a warm, relaxing bath. Or sit down in front of the fire with an entertaining book. The chances are that the best solution will be quite clear to you after an interval of an hour or so. Your subconscious mind will have continued

to work on the problem and will have produced a solution for you.

3   When you're looking for a solution to a major problem, try writing down a string of possible answers. Scribble them down just as fast as you possibly can. Do this for ten or fifteen minutes or so and then sit down and look at what you've produced. You'll find that many of the things you've written down still look silly or downright stupid. These can be discarded straight away. But many of the others will be useful. One of your jottings will very probably be the solution you're looking for.

4   If you want to try sharpening your powers of prediction, try guessing what are going to be the lead stories in tomorrow morning's newspapers. Or try guessing whose picture will appear on the cover of one of the weekly news magazines. Or try to predict the outcome of forthcoming sporting events or elections. Try to see a particular individual winning. Or try to see yourself holding a newspaper with the headline clearly visible. Remember that visual images are easier to play with than any other kind. So when you're trying this type of exercise always try to 'see' something happening, rather than trying to think about it in cold, analytical terms. If you try this type of technique regularly, your brain will become more and more efficient at sorting out information and coming up with instant answers – your intuitive sense will be improved.

CHAPTER 8

Knowing your own mind

Everyone has mindpower. The questionnaires on the following pages are designed to help you decide how to make the best possible use of your personal strengths, how best to conquer your weaknesses and how to use the mindpower techniques which are likely to be most useful to you.

Do you let enough laughter into your life?
To find out answer these questions with a 'yes' or 'no'.

1 Do you find it difficult to laugh at yourself?
2 Do you get cross if you are in an important meeting and someone starts to tell a joke or funny story?
3 Would you be deeply offended if you did something silly and people laughed at you?
4 Do you prefer watching serious documentaries to light comedy films?
5 Do you think that your position or status means that you need to behave in a serious manner when in public?
6 Do you think cartoon books and comic magazines are a waste of time?
7 Do you think that sex and humour should be kept apart?
8 Would you be embarrassed to laugh out loud in a hospital or church?
9 Do you think that practical jokes are invariably childish?
10 Do you think people who laugh a lot are immature?

Now check your score.
If you answered 'yes' to four or fewer questions, humour plays a sensible part in your life. If you answered 'yes' to five or

more questions, there is probably too little laughter in your life. Laughter can offer protection as well as providing a healing force.

Has your life got purpose?
To find out whether or not you need more purpose in your life answer 'yes' or 'no' to the following questions.

1 Do you ever feel that something is lacking in your life?
2 Are you frequently bored?
3 Do you have any unfulfilled ambitions?
4 Do you wish you had more responsibility?
5 Do you sometimes think that you are wasting your life?
6 Are you doing what you dreamt of doing when you were eighteen years old?
7 Do you look forward to the future?
8 Do you wish you were extended more often?
9 Have you got any talent or skills which are not fully employed?
10 Are you proud of your achievements?

Now check your score.
1 Yes: 1 point; No: 0 points
2 Yes: 1 point; No: 0 points
3 Yes: 0 points; No: 1 point
4 Yes: 1 point; No: 0 points
5 Yes: 1 point; No: 0 points
6 Yes: 0 points; No: 1 point
7 Yes: 0 points; No: 1 point
8 Yes: 1 point; No: 0 points
9 Yes: 1 point; No: 0 points
10 Yes: 0 points; No: 1 point

If you scored 7 to 10 points, you definitely need more purpose in your life. At the moment your failure to satisfy the simplest of your ambitions means that you are frustrated and bored; both can be damaging and destructive forces which can produce physical and mental disorders. If you scored 4 to 6 points, you are not so dangerously short of satisfaction. But you are still at risk of disease and damage from boredom and frustration. Your life needs purpose. If you scored 3 or less, your life is rich in purpose and you seem likely to satisfy some if if not all of your ambitions. At least you will have tried.

Are you floating on optimism – or sunk by pessimism?
Answer 'yes' or 'no' to these ten questions to find out whether you are an optimist, a pessimist or a comfortable mixture of the two.

1 Do you ever bet?
2 Do you ever dream about what you'd do if you suddenly came into a large sum of money?
3 Do you routinely carry a safety pin with you in case something breaks?
4 If you heard a knock on the door late at night, would you assume that it meant either bad news or trouble of some sort?
5 You get a Valentine card but you don't know who it is from. Would you assume that it was a joke from a friend rather than a message from an unknown admirer?
6 Would you ever go away without making hotel reservations beforehand?
7 Do you regularly spend money on insurance of one sort or another?
8 When you're going out, do you always carry a macintosh or umbrella?
9 If your doctor arranged for you to see a hospital consultant, would you assume that something serious must be wrong?
10 Would you catch an earlier train than necessary if you had an important appointment?

Now check your score.
1 Yes: 1 point; No: 0 points
2 Yes: 1 point; No: 0 points
3 Yes: 0 points; No: 1 point
4 Yes: 0 points; No: 1 point
5 Yes: 0 points; No: 1 point
6 Yes: 1 point; No: 0 points
7 Yes: 0 points; No: 1 point
8 Yes: 0 points; No: 1 point
9 Yes: 0 points; No: 1 point
10 Yes; 0 points; No: 1 point

If you scored between 7 and 10 points, you are an absolute optimist. Your approach to life should ensure that your health is not adversely affected by your attitude towards minor problems and troubles. (Although you should be aware that if your attitude became too cavalier, you could find yourself in tremendous trouble one day.) If you scored 4 or less points, you are an absolute pessimist. Your approach to health will probably affect your health adversely and you should try to modify your naturally pessimistic feelings. If you scored 4, 5 or 6 points, you are fairly well balanced but you could undoubtedly enhance your health by learning how to deal with your ups and downs in a more optimistic way.

Are you so cool that your health is suffering?
Answer 'yes' or 'no' to these questions.

1 Do you touch someone you love at least once every day?
2 Do you enjoy physical signs of affection?
3 Do you regularly tell those you love just how you feel about them?
4 Do you enjoy being kissed and hugged by people you love?
5 Do you dislike sleeping alone?
6 Have you ever had a pet of which you were very fond?
7 Do you enjoy being massaged?
8 Would you happily hold hands in public with someone you cared for?
9 Do you think women should be encouraged to breastfeed babies in public?
10 Do you ever get broody when you see small babies?

Now add up your score.
If you answered 'yes' to less than 5 questions, you are a rather cool individual and you should make more effort to allow yourself to care for others. Even more important, you should try to let yourself show your affection without feeling guilty or embarrassed. If you answered 'yes' to 5 or more questions, you are already a very caring person with few problems in this area. The more 'yes' answers you scored, the safer you are.

Have you got your priorities right?
Read through these questions carefully. There are no right or wrong answers. But by asking yourself these questions you

will learn a great deal about your ability to differentiate between the important things in your life and the trivia.

1 Do you know what things are important in your life?
2 Do you always make sure that those things take precedence over other areas of your life?
3 Do you find it easy to delegate responsibility for minor problems?
4 Do you ever waste time worrying about trivial problems?
5 How far would you go to protect or further the priorities in your life?
6 What things in your life give you the greatest happiness?
7 What things in your life make you most miserable?
8 How much time do you spend on those things that give you happiness?
9 How much time do you spend on those things that make you miserable?
10 Which individuals contribute most to your happiness?
11 Which individuals contribute most to your unhappiness?
12 How much time do you spend with the people you care about most?
13 How much time do you spend with people you don't really like?
14 How much time do you spend enjoying yourself?
15 How important is money to you?
16 How much time do you spend making money?
17 How important is your work?
18 How much time do you spend worrying about your work?
19 How important to you are your possessions?
20 How much time do you spend making money to buy possessions?
21 How important are your hobbies?
22 How much time do you spend on your hobbies?
23 What is your most important ambition?
24 How could you best improve the quality of your life?
25 What priorities do the people who are close to you have?

Do you need to assert yourself more?

Answer these questions to find out whether or not you need to be more assertive. Answer all the questions with a 'yes' or a 'no' and then add up the total number of 'yes' points that you have scored.

1 Do you ever find yourself accepting invitations that you'd really rather turn down?
2 Do you sit on any committees that you consider to be a waste of time?
3 Do you ever go out to dinner or to see friends when you'd rather have a quiet evening at home?
4 Would you feel guilty if you let the telephone ring without answering it?
5 Have you ever lent anyone money (or anything else) because you didn't like to say 'no'?
6 When watching television do you invariably end up watching what someone else wants to watch?
7 If a waiter was rude to you, would you put up with his behaviour rather than complain?
8 Do you ever buy things that you don't really want because you don't like to disappoint the salesman?
9 Do you ever take holidays in places you don't really like?
10 Do you ever spend Christmas with people you don't get on with particularly well?

Now check your score.
If you scored between 7 and 10 'yes' points, your lack of self-confidence is very likely to be having an adverse effect on your health. You need to assert yourself more and take greater control of your life. If you scored between 3 and 6 'yes' points you still probably need to assert yourself a little more. If you scored 2 or fewer 'yes' points, you are unlikely to need advice on how to assert yourself.

Do you have a healthy attitude towards crying?
Answer these questions to find out whether or not your attitude to crying is a healthy one. Simply answer 'yes' or 'no' to each question.

1 Do you feel guilty if you cry in public?
2 Do you think that crying is usually a sign of weakness?
3 Do you think that boys should be encouraged to hide their tears?
4 Do you feel embarrassed if you cry while watching a film or reading a book with a sensitive theme?
5 Would you try to hold back your tears if attending a funeral or some other sad event?

6 Would you distrust a leader who shed tears in public?
7 Would you pretend that you had something in your eye if you were unexpectedly discovered crying?
8 Do you get embarrassed if you see grown men crying?
9 Would you allow someone to comfort you if you were found crying?
10 Do you think tears are an unnecessary expression of emotion?

Now check your score.
If you scored three or more 'yes' points your attitude to crying is not healthy. Crying is a natural response and suppressing tears is storing up trouble for yourself.

Is anger damaging your health?
To find out just how susceptible you are to anger answer 'yes' or 'no' to these questions.

1 Do you always try to hide your anger?
2 Do you tend to stay angry for long periods of time?
3 Does your temper ever get out of control?
4 Do you suffer from physical symptoms (headaches, stomach pains, etc) when you are angry?
5 Do you always try to resist the temptation to complain if you are angry about something?
6 Do you get cross quite often?
7 Do you tend to brood about things which have made you angry?
8 Do you have difficulty in getting to sleep after something has annoyed you?
9 Does your face go red (or white) when you get angry?
10 Have you ever got into trouble because of your anger?

Now check your score.
If you answered 'yes' between 7 and 10 times, you do need to learn to control your anger. If you scored 4 to 6 'yes' points, anger is less likely to produce problems. If you scored 3 or fewer 'yes' points, anger is unlikely to be a major force in your life; nor is it likely to cause you any physical or mental damage.

Do you need to be ill?
To find out whether or not you use any illness as a weapon or excuse just answer 'yes' or 'no' to the following questions.

148

1 Do you suffer from any symptoms which disappear and reappear at apparently irregular and unexpected intervals?
2 Do you have any long-term medical problem for which your doctor has been unable to find any explanation?
3 When you were small, did you ever use physical symptoms of any kind to enable you to stay away from school?
4 Have you ever felt secretly pleased when you've developed an illness which has enabled you to avoid some unpleasant social event?
5 When you were ill as a child, did your mother make a tremendous fuss of you?
6 Do you enjoy being looked after when you are ill?
7 Do you regularly have to miss important but unpleasant appointments through ill health?
8 Do you invariably develop mild physical symptoms (such as nausea, diarrhoea, muscular pains, etc.) when you are under pressure or stressed?
9 Has anyone ever accused you of malingering?
10 Do you tend to retire to your bed if you are upset, worried or anxious?

Now check your score.
If you answered 'yes' to 7 or more questions, it is very likely that you (probably unconsciously) regularly use symptoms of ill health to enable you to avoid unpleasant confrontations or threatening experiences. The real problem with using ill health in this way is that you are never likely to get healthy as long as you *need* your illness. If you answered 'yes' to between 4 and 7 questions, it is possible that you use ill health as a weapon. If you answered 'yes' to 3 or fewer questions, it is unlikely that you use ill health as a weapon.

Do you need more excitement in your life?
Read through these questions carefully and answer 'yes' or 'no' to them all.

1 Do you think that you are in a rut?
2 Do you regularly get bored?
3 Do you wish that you had more responsibility?
4 Do you regularly spend time operating machinery over which you have little or no control?

5 Do you usually know what you are going to do each day?
6 Do your partner's habits regularly get on your nerves?
7 Does television provide most of the highlights in your life?
8 Is your partner totally predictable in bed?
9 Do you wish there were more surprises in your life?
10 Do you envy people who live exciting lives?

Now add up your score.
If you scored 7 or more 'yes' points, you are suffering badly from boredom. You desperately need to add more excitement to your life. If you scored between 4 and 6 'yes' points, boredom is a fairly major driving force affecting your health. You should do something to combat your boredom. If you scored 3 or less, boredom is unlikely to play an important part in your life.

Do you need to be more self-confident?

To find out how much your life is damaged by a lack of self-confidence read these questions carefully and answer 'yes' or 'no' to them all.

1 Do you usually avoid doing things that might upset other people – even if they are things that you'd like to do?
2 Do you feel bad if you go into a shop and come out without having bought anything?
3 Do you invariably dress to please other people?
4 Do you spend a lot of your life doing things that you don't enjoy?
5 Do you feel guilty if you really enjoy yourself?
6 Do you let other people run your life for you?
7 Do you think that you have far more weaknesses than strengths?
8 Do you worry a lot if you accidentally upset other people?
9 Do you regularly find yourself apologizing to other people?
10 Do you often find yourself wishing that you had more skills and talents?

Now check your score.
If you answered 'yes' to 7 or more questions, you are desperately in need of more confidence. Your lack of self-assurance is undoubtedly having an adverse affect on your health. If you answered 'yes' to 3 to 6 questions, it is still quite

likely that your lack of self-confidence is affecting your health. If you answered 'yes' to 2 or less questions, your health is unlikely to be damaged by any lack of confidence you may feel.

How do your relationships with others affect your health?

Make a list of all the people with whom you have close and important relationships. Now, beginning with the top name on your list, answer the questions which follow. Then repeat the questions for each other individual on your list. The answers to your questions will help you understand your relationships with others a little better.

1 Who is the stronger partner in your relationship?
2 Do you tend to lean on him/her a great deal?
3 Does he/she tend to lean on you a great deal?
4 Do you tend to take him/her for granted a good deal?
5 Does he/she tend to take you for granted?
6 Can you always rely on him/her when you need help?
7 Can he/she always rely on you when he/she needs help?
8 Does he/she ever intimidate or frighten you?
9 Do you think you ever intimidate or frighten him/her?
10 Is he/she dependent on you for money?
11 Are you dependent on him/her for money?
12 Would you trust him/her with money or important possessions?
13 Do you think that he/she would trust you with money or important possessions?
14 Do you like him/her?
15 Do you love him/her?
16 Do you think he/she likes you?
17 Do you think he/she loves you?
18 What do you gain from your relationship?
19 What does he/she gain from your relationship?
20 Do you always talk kindly about him/her when he/she is not present?
21 Do you think he/she always talks kindly about you when you are absent?
22 What are his/her greatest ambitions?
23 What are his/her greatest fears?
24 What do you think is the most important thing in his/her life?

25 If your car broke down at 3 in the morning, would you be able to ring him/her and ask for help?
26 If his/her car broke down at 3 in the morning, would he/she be able to ring you and ask for help?
27 Does he/she benefit financially from your relationship?
28 Do you benefit financially from your relationship?
29 What annoys you most about him/her?
30 What do you think annoys him/her most about you?

There are no correct answers to these questions. But if you think about your answers carefully, you may find that you will learn something about your relationships with and your attitudes to other people.

How tranquil are you?

These questions are designed to help you find out just how vulnerable your mind is to stress and pressure – and how much you would benefit from learning how to relax your mind. Answer 'yes' or 'no' to all these questions and then add up the total number of 'yes' answers that you have scored.

1 Do you get easily irritated?
2 Do you ever suffer from 'panic' attacks?
3 Do you find it difficult to relax?
4 Do you wish you had less responsibility?
5 Do you find yourself getting frustrated a good deal?
6 Do you need tranquillizers or sleeping tablets to help you deal with stress or pressure?
7 Do you ever feel like packing it all in and running away?
8 Do you suffer from any symptoms which are caused by or made worse by pressure?
9 Would you describe yourself as a 'worrier'?
10 Do you always seem to be in a hurry?

If you scored 7 to 10 'yes' points, you would benefit enormously from learning how to relax your mind. You are extremely susceptible to stress, pressure, anxiety and worry. If you scored 4 to 6 'yes' points, you are far less susceptible to worry and stress. But you would still benefit from learning how to relax your mind. If you scored 3 or less 'yes' points, you are fairly strong. But you might still benefit from studying the pages dealing with tranquillity.

How physically tense are you?

The questions below are designed to help you find out just how vulnerable your body is to stress and pressure – and to show how important it is that you learn how to relax your body properly. Simply answer 'yes' or 'no' to all these questions and then add up the total number of 'yes' answers that you score.

1 When you are excited do you ever have difficulty in breathing or do you ever wheeze?
2 When you are angry does your face ever go red?
3 When you are frightened or anxious do you sweat?
4 Do you ever get butterflies in your stomach?
5 Do you ever suffer from palpitations when you are anxious or upset?
6 Do you ever suffer from vomiting or diarrhoea before important occasions?
7 Does your pulse ever race when you are excited?
8 Do you ever develop a rash when you are excited or nervous?
9 Do you ever get headaches when you are worried?
10 Have you ever fainted when you've been frightened?

The number of times you answered 'yes' indicates the extent to which your body responds to mental stresses and pressures. If you continue to remain exposed to stress and pressure without learning how to protect yourself, you will eventually develop symptoms and signs of stress-induced illness. (The questions you have answered above will probably help you determine the type of problems that are most likely to worry you.) To protect yourself you must learn to relax your body.

A score of 7 to 10 'yes' points indicates that your body is particularly susceptible to stress and pressures. A score of 3 to 6 'yes' points is average. A score of 2 or fewer 'yes' points indicates that you are less vulnerable than most individuals to physical problems produced by stress.

How well developed is your imagination?

Read through the questions below. And answer them 'yes' or 'no'.

1 Do you ever dream while you are asleep?
2 Did you ever daydream as a child?
3 Have you ever had a nightmare?

4 Do you ever fantasize about people you know or about film stars or celebrities?
5 Have you ever had a feeling of *déjà vu*? (thinking that you have been somewhere before, when in reality it is your first visit).
6 Do you ever fantasize when making love?
7 Do you have any strong religious beliefs?
8 Do you ever get frightened when watching horror movies?
9 Do you ever wonder what it would have been like to live in a different century?
10 Do you ever worry about your loved ones' safety when they are travelling?

The more times you answered 'yes', the greater the power of your imagination. But as long as you answered 'yes' at least once, your imagination is powerful enough to be used as a healing force.

How strong is your sense of intuition?
Answer 'yes' or 'no' to the following questions.

1 Do you tend to do well in guessing games?
2 Have you ever had a long run of good luck when gambling?
3 Have you ever known what was in a letter before opening it?
4 Have you ever had bad dreams which turned out to be true?
5 Have you ever thought about someone you haven't heard from and then, out of the blue, received a telephone call, postcard or letter from them? Or met them unexpectedly in the street?
6 Do you ever know what people are going to say before they say it?
7 Have you ever heard voices telling you what to do?
8 Have you ever 'known' who was on the other end before picking up a ringing telephone?
9 Have you ever felt that a house was right for you the moment you saw it?
10 Have you ever felt that you wanted to know someone better after seeing them for no more than an instant?

Now add up your score.

If you answered 'yes' to at least one question, you have intuitive powers that you could use to your advantage. The greater your score, the greater your powers.

Putting mindpower into perspective

The strength of mindpower lies in its simplicity. The aim is to enable you to conquer the powers that cause illness and then to turn those powers round to produce good health. You cannot change your personality and you may not be able to change your circumstances. But you can change the way that you allow your personality and your environment to interact; that is the simple strength of mindpower.

Follow the mindpower philosophy and you will benefit in two distinct ways: when you are well you'll be less likely to fall ill; and when you are ill you'll be more likely to get well.

There are two final points which I think are worth stressing. First, mindpower is not an alternative to orthodox medicine. Eventually, I hope that mindpower will encourage patients to think of health care in an entirely different way. I believe that we as individuals must take more responsibility for our bodies and our minds. But mindpower will not replace medical treatment. There will always be a place for doctors and healers; they are needed as technicians, to be called as aides and assistants in the fight for good health and happiness. Mindpower offers a new approach, a new philosophy, a new dimension and a new priority.

Second, mindpower is essentially a philosophy designed for the individual. When I first started talking about the idea of mindpower, I was delighted to find that it was accepted with tremendous enthusiasm by just about everyone with whom I came into contact. But, at the same time, I was horrified when several people wanted to turn mindpower into a genuine form of 'alternative medicine'. Two separate individuals wanted to launch a chain of mindpower clinics across Britain – with Vernon Coleman as resident guru. Another, more ambitious,

wanted a chain of clinics around the world.

They had missed the point. Mindpower offers an opportunity for you the reader to take charge of your own life, to look
after your own medical destiny and to take back some of the responsibility which has, in recent years, been taken from you by traditional interventionists.

There will be no mindpower clinics, no mindpower products, and no mindpower practitioners. Mindpower is an idea, an approach and a philosophy of life. It is a book. No more and no less. But I hope it will change your life.

Mindpower in practice – mental self-defence

These sections are designed to give you some practical examples of how the principles of mindpower can be used.

Although you can use mindpower to help you deal with well over 90 per cent of all symptoms and diseases, there are obviously problems which do need interventionist help. In general, I suggest that you seek help from a professional if you have any severe or uncontrollable pain, any unexplained pain which recurs or which is present for more than five days, any unexplained bleeding, any persistent changes in your body or in any existing lump, wart or skin blemish, any new symptoms which develop after receiving medical treatment, or any severe mental symptoms such as confusion, paranoia, disorientation or severe depression. If you are in any doubt about the diagnosis, I strongly suggest that you visit a registered medical practitioner for a preliminary assessment of your condition.

But do not forget that, even when a problem needs the attention of a health professional, you can still use mindpower to help improve your strength and rate of healing. Mindpower has an important part to play in your self-preservation programme too. If you constantly see yourself as ill and weak, you will become ill and weak. If you constantly see yourself as strong, supple and healthy, your chances of being strong, supple and healthy will be improved immeasurably. If you spend your days expecting your joints to become arthritic because your parents suffered from arthritis, the chances are that your joints will become arthritic. If, however, you see your joints as smooth and pain-free, the chances are that they will remain smooth and pain-free.

Finally, remember that the following sections are designed only to provide you with an introduction to the ways in which you can use your mindpower. In order to benefit fully from mindpower I suggest that you reread Chapters 5,6 and 7 and then apply the principles to your particular problems.

Accidents

If you are worrying about something that happened at work and you fail to see a red light, is that really an accident? If you are upset because of a problem with a loved one and you step out in front of a bus, is that really an accident? If you are thinking about your financial problems rather than what you're doing and you scald yourself in the kitchen, can that really be described as an unavoidable accident? I don't think so. Stress, pressure and anxiety are all major causes of accidental injury. And in many cases the accident could have been prevented.

Indeed it is, I think, quite safe to say that the majority of accidents aren't truly accidental at all. They don't occur because of completely unforeseen circumstances, but because someone has been careless or ignorant or, even more commonly, because someone has been unable to concentrate because of worry or anxiety produced by some outside problem.

If you seem to be accident-prone, so well known that the staff in your local casualty department greet you by your first name, you can use mindpower to help you avoid accidents in two quite different ways.

If you are accident-prone, the chances are that you are forever beseiged by a host of small problems. Your mind is probably always so busy trying to sort things out that you are never able to concentrate properly on what you're supposed to be doing. You will, therefore, be able to help yourself considerably by trying to put the things that are worrying you into some sort of perspective.

Begin by making a list of all the things that are worrying you and dividing the list into several different categories. So, for example, you might have lists of problems that worry you at home, problems that worry you at work and problems that worry you in your relationships.

Next, try to look at each of these problems in turn and decide whether – and exactly how – worrying about them will change things. Try to decide what you can do about each problem and where you can take some action, then do so. You'll probably be surprised to find that many of the problems which seem very significant when allowed to trouble you unexamined will be far less devastating when examined in close detail.

The other thing that you can do to help yourself avoid accidents is to try and improve your sense of intuition. If you can do this, you will at the same time improve your reflexes and the way that you respond to threats and dangers of all kinds. Although the word intuition seems to suggest something quite unearthly and irrational, the fact is that we base intuitive responses on things that we have learned.

You can, therefore, improve your sense of intuition by taking notice of everything about you. Make sure, for instance, that you know as much as you are ever likely to need to know about the machines you operate and the cars you drive. You should also make sure that you know as much as possible about the places where you live and work. So, for example, if you know that the nearest fire extinguisher to your office is on the landing between the two lifts, you'll instinctively go there if a fire breaks out. It will seem like intuition or instinct, but it will be little more than plain common sense based on practical knowledge.

Mindpower can't prevent all accidents, of course. There will occasionally be incidents which will be totally outside your control. But if you think about it carefully, you'll soon see that the vast majority of accidents can be prevented.

And even when accidents do happen, you can still use mindpower to improve your chances of getting well quickly. Once again the value of mindpower has to be put into perspective, of course. If you have a broken leg, you'll need to have the bones set, you'll probably need a splint or plaster cast for the leg and you'll need specialist advice from an orthopaedic consultant and a physiotherapist. But by using mindpower you will be able to speed up the rate of your recovery. There are several ways in which you can help yourself.

1   Try to remain as hopeful and as positive as possible if you do suffer injury. Suppose you fall down while skiing. If you immediately decide that you have broken your leg, that it is going to go septic, that it will probably need amputating and that you will undoubtedly be disabled for the rest of your life, by the time that you arrive in the local casualty department your body will have reacted, not to the fall you've just had, but to the major threat that you have imagined. Your muscles will be tense, the pain will be enormous and your heart rate and blood pressure will have reacted, not to the real problem that you've acquired (possibly a fairly minor one), but to the problem that you've started worrying about (a major one).

If, on the other hand, you find that, although it hurts, you can stand and walk and you tell yourself that you've simply bruised some tissues and you'll take things a little carefully for a while, you'll suffer far less pain and far less immobility. If instead of 'seeing' yourself in a hospital bed you see yourself recovering in no time and winning the Olympic downhill gold medal, you'll get over your accident far more speedily.

2   The amount of attention you give to an injury will be influenced by the importance of whatever else is in your mind at the same time. If you are concentrating hard on something which is important to you, your injury may well go virtually unnoticed. People playing sport, for example, can often injure themselves seriously without

160

being aware of the injury. In one famous Cup Final football match a goalkeeper carried on playing unaware that he had broken his neck.

If you have banged your arm while gardening, give it a good rub, check that you haven't broken anything or cut yourself and then get yourself interested in the next job you'd planned. Your injury will be far less serious than it might otherwise have been.

3 If after an injury you succeed in relaxing your mind and your body, your body's natural healing response will take over, your body's responses to the injury will not be exaggerated and the pain and discomfort that you feel will be minimized.

So, if you have a serious injury which necessitates a stay in hospital or simply a stay in bed, try to relax your mind by daydreaming. Allow your mind to wander from your sick bed to enjoy a day on the beach or a day in the country or whatever else you find relaxing. *See* pages 128–30.

4 Laughter helps eradicate pain and heal damaged tissues. So, if your accident results in a stay in bed, make sure that you have a good supply of entertaining books and magazines to read and funny films and videos to watch.

5 Pains that accompany injuries can often be relieved by using imagery techniques. So, for example, relax yourself completely and then imagine that the pains which are worrying you are being transmitted around your body through a series of thin wires. Then imagine that a team of tiny physicians are wandering around your body cutting all the wires they can find. Take the team of wire-cutting medics to each painful part of your body in turn.

Remember, I'm not suggesting that any of these techniques alone will mend your broken bones or heal your damaged body. You may still need professional medical help. But by using mindpower, you will improve the speed with which you get better and you will reduce the risk of complications developing.

Anxiety and Depression

Mental diseases are becoming more and more common. In America, the National Institutes of Mental Health recently conducted a $15 million survey that lasted six years and arrived at the startling conclusion that one in every six American adults suffers from at least one psychiatric ailment. And the commonest ailments suffered were anxiety and depression. Similar figures would be obtained if surveys were done in Britain, France, Germany, Scandinavia, Australia or just about any other so-called 'developed' country.

There are, of course, times when depression does need specialist psychiatric help. There are some types of depression which are difficult to treat, which require hospital treatment and which may last for considerable periods of time. But the majority of patients suffering from anxiety or depression do not need specialist help or in-patient therapy. And of all the common medical problems, these two states of mind are probably the two most badly treated by general practitioners.

The usual response is, I fear, for a general practitioner to prescribe tranquillizers of one sort or another. And they are neither an effective short-term solution, nor a safe and satisfactory long-term answer. Around the world tranquillizer addiction is now a major medical problem. It is, indeed, the world's biggest drug addiction problem. Figures vary from country to country, but on average something like one in every ten individuals takes a benzodiazepine – a drug such as Valium, Librium and Mogadon. In Britain alone there are hundreds of thousands of men and women (mainly women) who have been taking tranquillizers for several years and who can confirm that these drugs do not offer a safe solution.

The mindpower philosophy does, however, offer a number of effective remedies for individuals who are suffering from anxiety or depression and who want to learn how to deal with their symptoms permanently and safely. These same remedies, incidentally, will help those individuals currently trying to wean themselves off benzo-diazepine tranquillizers.

1 People who suffer from depression or who suffer from anxiety often lack self-assurance. If you feel that a lack of self-confidence could be contributing to your problem, try to restore your faith in yourself by thinking of all your virtues. Imagine that you are a good friend and try to describe yourself from afar, from an enthusiastic point of view. You'll probably be amazed to find out just how many hidden virtues you have got.

2 Use your imagination to help build up your confidence. Most people who suffer from anxiety make things far worse for themselves by forever imagining the worst.

A patient of mine called Olive worked as a shop assistant in a large department store. When the post of floor supervisor became vacant, she desperately wanted to apply. But every time she went up to the personnel office to fill in an application form she got cold feet. She thought that they would probably laugh at her for applying and in her mind could see them having a good giggle behind her back. She felt certain that they wouldn't treat her application seriously.

In the end she got into quite a state about it. She even considered complaining to the store manager about what she imagined the personnel office would say about her. Her problem, of course, was that she had absolutely no confidence in herself or her abilities. And her lack of confidence was crippling her chances of getting the job she

162

so desperately wanted. She couldn't 'see' herself being successful. But she could 'see' herself failing very clearly.

Eventually I managed to persuade her to try substituting her negative image of herself with a much more positive one. I told her to spend a few minutes every morning and every evening just imagining herself handing in her application form, being interviewed by the personnel manager and doing the job of floor supervisor.

After a week, during which she had bombarded her mind with a series of very positive images, Olive successfully managed to hand in her application. To her surprise the clerk in the personnel office said they'd been waiting for her to apply and had wondered why she hadn't applied before. Ten days later Olive got the job.

3   Many people who suffer with their 'nerves' find it difficult to express their feelings – they tend to bottle things up inside them. This can be very harmful.

Try, therefore, to get into the habit of letting your emotions flow quite freely from time to time. If you feel like getting angry, let your anger out. You don't have to shout or have a tantrum in a shop, but let the manager know if you are dissatisfied with a product you've bought or with the service you've had. Write a strong letter of complaint to the company's managing director and post it – don't just leave it lying on the mantelpiece. You'll benefit not just by getting rid of your anger but also by building up your self-confidence and self-esteem. You'll begin to see yourself as someone who can't be 'sat' upon or abused so freely.

If you do feel your anger building up inside you and eating away at you, do something physical to get rid of the accumulating tension. Go for a good, brisk walk, for example. It really is possible to 'walk off' an angry feeling. If you feel very upset about something, let your emotions show. Don't be afraid to cry. Sobbing can often make you feel a good deal fitter and stronger. And be prepared to share your sorrow with someone else too.

Some people who suffer from anxiety or depression say that they can't share their state of mind because they haven't got any good friends. In fact, it is often because they don't share their emotional feelings that they don't have any good friends. Friendship is all about sharing – telling people about things that have upset you and listening when they tell you about things which have upset them. Start talking, start sharing and you'll find that you do have friends.

4   Take a good, close look at your relationships with others. Are there any people at work who annoy you or upset you? Do you get annoyed by relatives? If so, ask yourself why things are so wrong. Whose fault is it? What can you do to heal the rift? Do you need to heal the rift or can you just avoid seeing them? Remember, just because people are relatives, you won't necessarily like them or be

able to get on with them.

5 Learn to laugh. Does your life need more fun? Are you too serious? Many people feel that it is childish to have fun, to play games, to enjoy a laugh or to squander time on entertainment. Maybe it is. But it's healthy to laugh and to have fun. Visit a local joke shop or toy shop and see what memories are stimulated. Buy books and magazines that you find entertaining and amusing rather than just educational. Start watching entertaining programmes on television – or try hiring a good video occasionally. If you are hiring a video film, invite one or two friends round to enjoy it with you.

6 Spend a little time daydreaming. If the weather is cold and wet and you're feeling miserable, lie back, close your eyes and imagine that you're on a beach having a splendid time. Visit your local travel agent and pick up a collection of holiday brochures. Look through the illustrations, find a picture that takes your fancy and imagine that you're there, soaking up the sun. *See* pages 128–30.

Arthritis

Few diseases affect as many people as arthritis, few cause as much pain, discomfort and disablement and few are the subject of so many myths and so much misunderstanding. In fact, the first myth to get out of the way is the idea that there is any such thing as a single disease called arthritis. The word 'arthritis' is about as useful and specific as the word 'infection', and just as there are over a hundred different types of infection so there are over a hundred different types of arthritis. These different forms of arthritis vary enormously in the amount of damage and crippling they produce and in the length of time they are likely to last.

The second important point is that, although arthritis is usually incurable, it is invariably possible to minimize the symptoms produced. The diseases which are collectively known as 'arthritis' do not kill and, if treated with respect rather than fear, it is possible to reduce the amount of damage they do.

Whether an individual's arthritis has been caused or made worse by strain, ageing, wear and tear, genetic susceptibility, infection with a bacterium or a virus, injury, a metabolic or chemical abnormality or a hormonal abnormality, the symptoms will get worse if they are left untreated or treated half-heartedly. If, on the other hand, treatment is initiated early and with enthusiasm, the outlook can be greatly improved.

By using the knowledge which has been acquired over the last few decades, it is possible to prevent the destruction of the body's joints and the associated crippling, to relieve joint pain and stiffness, to

164

restore lost joint function and slow down, or even halt, the rate at which arthritis affects the body. And although it is perfectly true that some of the treatments used for arthritis have been shown to have dangerous side-effects, it is equally true that there are millions of patients around the world who have been treated quite safely by drugs, surgery and physiotherapy.

While I think that it is important to stress the value of obtaining proper orthodox medical advice for any arthritic condition, I am also sure that mindpower has a valuable part to play in the treatment of these conditions. Arthritis, like so many other types of disease, is not simply a mechanical problem. The physical symptoms produced by the joint changes which characterize arthritic disorders are known to be exacerbated by anxiety, pressure, stress and worry.

We know that arthritis is probably a disorder produced by changes in the body's immune system. And we know that the body's immune system can be affected by the mind. We know that arthritis is affected by an individual's personality. We know that arthritis is an inflammatory disorder and we know that inflammatory disorders are made worse by anxiety. We know that the type of muscle tension produced by nervousness can make arthritic pains and deformities worse by having a simple, mechanical effect on the muscles and therefore on the bones and joints. But just how stress makes arthritis worse and just how all these effects interreact is still something of a mystery.

What we also know, however, is that the symptoms produced by arthritic changes can be relieved by using mindpower. Mindpower alone won't produce a marvellous 'wonder' cure (although it is far more likely to do so than any therapeutic solution). But it will, whether used alone or in conjunction with other prescribed remedies, relieve symptoms, help banish pain and help restore lost mobility.

There are several ways in which mindpower can help sufferers from arthritis.

1   Start by learning how to relax your body. So, for example, if you get arthritic pains in your leg, you will be able to minimize those pains by learning how to relax the muscles of that leg.

Start by practising when your pains are at their least troublesome. And start with the smallest muscles in the area. With your left leg, for example, begin by curling up the toes of your left foot. Try to tighten the muscles of your foot as much as you possibly can. When the muscles really begin to hurt, deliberately and carefully allow them to relax. Try to feel the muscles stretching and becoming looser. Imagine a good, plentiful blood supply to the area pumping in plenty of fresh, refreshing oxygen.

Then do the same sort of thing with your left ankle. Move the ankle up and then down as far as it will go in both directions. Turn the ankle first to one side and then to the other side. Keep it in each position until the muscles become slightly uncomfortable and start to ache. And then deliberately and slowly relax the muscles of your ankle.

Gradually work your way up your leg, tightening and then relaxing all the muscles in turn. As you move upwards, you'll learn how your muscles feel when they are loose and relaxed. After practising this exercise, you'll be able to relax the muscles of your leg quite quickly – without going through the tensing and tightening stage at all. This you can do every morning and evening – and whenever the pains of your arthritis are troubling you.

2   People who suffer from arthritis often appear strong-willed and purposeful. But that is frequently a false front. Arthritis sufferers often lack confidence and self-assurance. If you think that you lack self-confidence, try to boost your opinion of yourself by making a list of all your virtues and strengths. Write out the sort of obituary for yourself that a really good friend might compose. Don't be modest. Write out a promotion leaflet for yourself that an advertising agency might prepare. Think of yourself as the product and then try to sell yourself to the world.

3   Use the power of your mind to help combat the pains in your joints. You may not be able to get rid of your arthritic pains completely in this way, but you will certainly be able to reduce the amount of pain and reduce your dependence on analgesic drugs.

Try to see inside each joint that is painful. If, for example, you have pains in a hip joint, try to imagine that you have X-ray vision and you can see right inside the joint. See the raw edges of bone grating together uncomfortably, noisily and painfully. Now imagine that you can see an army of white-coated men inside that joint working hard to fill in all the cracks and crevices in the bony surfaces. They have a huge task before them, but it is a purely physical problem and one that can be overcome. Spend a few minutes visualizing the men working hard inside your joint. Imagine them as a team with a foreman supervising them and a series of experts offering specialist advice.

Then return to your image of the joint at frequent intervals during the day to check on the way that the work is progressing. Gradually the white-coated men will be able to repair the damage and reduce the amount of pain that you're suffering.

Alternatively, try to imagine that there is a central pain centre inside your brain. Now imagine that between all your joints and that central pain centre there are a number of pain-transmitting wires. Imagine that there is a wire from your left knee, one from your left hip, one from your right ankle and so on. Where you have joints that are pain-free the wires have already been cut, or have been broken. But where you have lots of pain the wires are clearly visible. Now cut each one of those wires in turn and prevent the pain messages getting to your pain centre.

Those are two examples of the ways in which you can use the mindpower technique of imagery to help yourself conquer pain. You can create new techniques that are tailor-made to suit your own imagination. So, if you enjoy cowboy films, substitute galloping cowboys for white-coated workers tackling the pains. If you like films or stories about science fiction, imagine that the pains in your joints are being produced by extra-terrestrial monsters. And imagine those pain-producing monsters being killed off by a fleet of tiny space craft inside you. *See* pages 133–7.

Asthma

I became very well aware of the close relationship between stress and asthma during my years working as a general practitioner. Time after time I saw both children and adults wheezing badly and struggling to breathe as a result of an accumulation of worries and fears. Children would sometimes start wheezing in response to their own anxieties – in the day or so prior to a school test or examination, for example. And sometimes their asthma would get worse in response to their parents' fears and anxieties. Adults would develop worsening symptoms of asthma as a result of domestic, occupational or social stresses.

As a short-term aid, I found that it was usually necessary to prescribe drugs designed to have a specific effect on the chest and to help relax the muscles controlling the breathing. In those instances where the asthma was produced or made worse by an allergy reaction, it was sometimes necessary to accompany the treatment with a drug designed to counter the allergy response. Where the problem was made worse by an infection, it was obviously necessary to prescribe an antibiotic too.

There are today a wide range of useful and extremely safe drugs available for the treatment of asthma. In addition to tablets to be taken by mouth or drugs requiring an injection, there are quite a number of products which can be administered simply through the aid of an inhaler. (Over the years I have met quite a number of patients who have become quite dependent on their inhalers. It is by no means unknown for asthma sufferers to start wheezing if they discover that they do not have an inhaler with them.)

But although these drugs are undoubtedly valuable, and although such products will continue to play a vital role in the treatment of asthma, I do believe that the link between pressures affecting the mind and the symptoms of asthma is so powerful that the principles of mindpower can in many cases be used with great effect.

Indeed, I have gradually become certain that the only real solution likely to offer any genuine long-term improvement is to be found through mindpower. Patients must be taught how to deal effectively with their own pressures and must learn how to protect themselves against the environmental circumstances most likely to exacerbate their own conditions. Many of the mindpower principles will help. The precise way in which the principles should be applied will invariably depend upon individual susceptibilities, but the notes which follow are intended to offer some basic guidance.

1   The typical wheezing of asthma develops because the muscles of the chest become constricted and air cannot easily get in and out of the lungs. The asthmatic makes a noise when breathing out for the same reason that air coming out of a balloon makes a noise if you pinch the neck with your fingers. Asthmatics can often relieve their symptoms by imagining that they can see the constricted tubes within their lungs and by then deliberately relaxing and opening those passageways.

Put baldly this sounds ridiculously simplistic, of course. But the fact is that it does work. The passageways which carry air into the lungs are tubes with muscles. And it is the tightening of those muscles which narrows them. Deliberately relaxing the muscles which encircle the air-carrying passageways is really no more difficult than deliberately relaxing the muscles of the hand or foot. All it takes is practice and the belief that it will work. And when you stop and think about it, there is absolutely no reason why it shouldn't work. After all if the muscles which regulate the size of the air-carrying tubes can be narrowed by stress, it is logical to assume that they can be widened by relaxation.

2   Asthma sufferers often benefit simply by learning how to relax their minds. A general state of relaxation affects the whole body – including the lungs.

To start you need to practise in a dark, quiet room. Disturbances and distractions can make things difficult. Then, while lying down comfortably, you should close your eyes and imagine that you are on a warm beach somewhere. Imagine that you can hear the waves breaking on the shore, that you can hear the seagulls overhead and that you can feel the warm sun on your face. The more convincing the daydream the more effective it will be as a relaxation aid. *See* also pages 128–30.

3   Individuals who suffer from asthma often have a considerable amount of difficulty in expressing their emotions. They bottle up anger and don't let themselves cry. That needs to change.

If you are an asthma sufferer try to make sure that you let out your anger whenever possible. If you are cross about something, let people know. You can still be polite and reasonable, but don't just bottle up your anger and frustrations inside you – they'll simply make things worse for you. Tell people you're cross. Tell people why you're cross. And expect solutions, answers and, where appropriate, apologies. As a final solution, remember that exercise is often a good way to get rid of anger. If you're feeling upset, go for a good, brisk walk.

Remember too that it is important to let yourself cry when you feel as if you want to. Don't keep your sorrow inside you – it will just do you damage and make your asthma worse. Let the tears out and don't be frightened to let people see that you are sad. If they are good friends, they are more likely to comfort you than to feel embarrassed.

4   People who suffer from asthma are sometimes deprived of love and affection – or even if they aren't they may think that they are. If you are an asthma sufferer and you feel that you need more 'love' in your life, ask yourself whether you are as loving as you could be. Do you tell your loved ones how you feel about them? Do you touch them as often as you could? Do you hug and cuddle them frequently? It may well be that you would receive more loving if you gave more.

If you are close to an asthma sufferer, try to show him or her as much affection as you possibly can – and encourage him or her to show you affection. People who suffer from asthma are often shy and easily embarrassed – they need bringing out of their shells.

Cancer

During the last few decades millions and millions of pounds have been spent by doctors searching for a cure for cancer. Many of their efforts have been designed to try and discover a single, pharmacological solution to what is, in fact, a whole range of different disorders.

The word 'cancer' is about as specific as the word 'infection' and covers a wide range of quite separate disorders. Just as it is unlikely that researchers will ever find a single drug answer to all infections, so it is unlikely that doctors will ever find a single drug answer to all cancers. In other words, although breakthroughs may be made in the treatment of individual cancers, it is unlikely that those breakthroughs will benefit sufferers from other types of cancer.

Doctors looking for a single solution have persisted with their rather irrational search for a variety of reasons – most of them economic or political, rather than scientific or medical. Cancer is an emotive word and it isn't difficult to raise money for a general cancer research programme. Not all doctors have, however, been looking for a single, wonder cure. In laboratories throughout the world researchers have made specific, but significant developments in the treatment of cancers. New drugs have been brought onto the market and great advances have been made in the development of radio-therapy techniques. It is these researchers who have had the greatest amount of success, and who have enabled doctors to improve the survival rate of patients suffering from such disorders as skin cancer and leukaemia.

Ironically, while orthodox researchers have been struggling unsuccessfully to produce a single drug remedy for cancer, there has been one tremendous advance made in the search for a single solution. And that advance has been made by researchers working, not in orthodox areas of medicine, but in the very unorthodox area linking the power of the mind to diseases of the body.

From the evidence of those who have been working in this valuable but under-financed medical backwater, it has become clear that there a number of very specific ways in which cancer sufferers can help themselves by using mindpower techniques.

Before describing these methods there is, however, one very important point which I must make. Some practitioners have suggested that the type of imagery technique which I have collected within the mindpower philosophy should be used in conjunction with other, alternative remedies such as vitamin therapy and laetrile (an extract from apricot kernels which has been widely tried and widely dismissed as being worthless). This is a dreadful pity. For although there is now irresistible evidence to show that the mindpower techniques can be used with very great effect by patients suffering from all types of cancer, there is no real evidence to suggest that special diets, vitamin therapy or laetrile have any useful effect.

There is, on the other hand, a considerable amount of evidence to show that to get the best possible results the mindpower techniques should be used in conjunction with orthodox medical techniques such as drug therapy or radiotherapy. If you are a cancer sufferer, your best chance of defeating your cancer lies in combining the orthodox weapons offered by doctors with the mental attitudes associated with mindpower. Neither method alone will have the power of these two approaches combined. And no other combi-nation of techniques is as effective as this one.

1 Learn to relax your mind as completely and as often as you possibly can. Prepare for yourself a small series of pleasant daydreaming scenarios and use those scenarios to help you deal with stressful circumstances and threatening situations. *See* pages 128–30.

2 Try to avoid too much contact with people who make you feel gloomy or depressed. And try to spend as much time as you can with

170

people who make you smile. Don't be frightened to laugh and enjoy yourself. We all have a limited lifespan on this earth. If we don't laugh and learn to enjoy ourselves, our lives are simply not worth living.

3   When you have learned to relax your mind thoroughly and completely, use your imagination to help you defeat your cancer. In the *Daily Mail* in June 1985 the actress Jill Ireland described how she used imagery techniques to help her fight cancer.

'I began visualizing cancer cells, then telling myself that cancer is a weak disease, composed of weak, confused, deformed cells . . . I visualized my white blood cells. I imagined them as piranha fish. They poured into the areas where the cancer cells were and destroyed them and I visualized them going around quietly and competently doing their job, taking care of my body and, if they saw any cancer cells they destroyed them.'

You can adapt this type of imagery technique to suit your own personal imagination. Think of your cancer cells as the baddies and of your body's defences as the goodies. Imagine your body's defences tearing around your body destroying the frightened cancer cells.

4   Learn to express your emotions. There is plenty of evidence available now to show that people who repress their anger and their tears are more likely to develop cancer and to succumb to it once they have developed it.

If you feel like crying, don't be afraid to cry. If you feel angry about something, don't be afraid to let your anger show. Share your emotional experiences with other people. The more you store up your emotions inside, the more damage those emotions are likely to do.

5   Assert yourself. If you are in hospital and the doctors and nurses won't tell you things that you feel you want to know, make a fuss and make a nuisance of yourself until they answer your questions.

Don't lie back and let the medical staff just do things to you. Insist on sharing in the care of your body. Insist on being consulted. Get out of bed if you really want to get out of bed. Watch television if you want to watch television. Eat a peanut butter sandwich at midnight if that is really what you want.

6   Built up your self-confidence. Learn to respect and value yourself as an individual. People who develop – and die of – cancer often have a low opinion of themselves. Build up your confidence and you'll live longer. *See* also pages 94–7.

Colds and Influenza

The officially recommended treatments for colds and influenza are

171

primitive and of limited value. Treating colds by prescribing substances designed to dry up secretions is rather like treating depression by prescribing something to dry up the tear ducts. And yet that, of course, is exactly what most doctors and pharmacists do.

What is offered as an apparent solution can, in fact, create problems of its own. There is now ample evidence to show that some of the products available on the market and widely used in the treatment of colds can, if used for more than a day or so, eventually produce exactly the same symptoms as the ones they were designed to counteract. If, for example, you use an inhaler to try and deal with your nasal congestion, you could end up with nasal congestion caused by your inhaler.

Nor are any of the other orthodox techniques of much value when it comes to dealing with a cold. Drugs such as penicillin don't work for the very simple but important reason that, whereas penicillin works by killing bacteria, colds are caused by a virus – an organism which is quite immune to penicillin and similar products.

Vaccines don't work because the common cold can be caused by any one of a couple of hundred different viruses and the chances of your being vaccinated against the right virus are remarkably slim. Indeed, since cold-producing viruses now travel around the world as fast as aeroplanes the chances are that the types of vaccine in one country will be quite out of date by the time they are made generally available.

The medical profession's failure to devise an effective remedy for the common cold (or indeed the 'flu virus) is largely due to the fact that, although a considerable amount of research work has been done on the subject, we still don't really know just how colds spread nor what makes particular individuals susceptible. We do know that infections seem to spread through the air and that the bugs which cause them seem to get into the body either through the mouth or through the eyes. And we know that many people who get colds do so because they touch their eyes with virus-carrying fingers which push the infection into the nearest tear duct. But we don't know why one individual will get a cold while another, seemingly exposed to an identical risk, will not.

What does seem clear is that our susceptibility to colds is enhanced by any sort of emotional imbalance. We get colds when we are frightened, worried, upset or nervous. We get colds when we are feeling low and expect to get them. We get colds before important functions or major occasions. And we get them when we are feeling uncertain about something. With all this information, how the bacteria which cause colds get into the body becomes almost irrelevant.

The answer is, it would seem, not to spend all our energies in trying

172

to find ways to interfere with the spread of infection nor to continue treating symptoms (itself a rather foolish activity since we now know that the naturally occurring mild fever and loss of appetite we have with a minor infection are produced to kill off the invading organism by exposing it to heat and a shortage of food supplies). Instead we should concentrate our efforts on using mindpower to improve our resistance to these minor forms of infection. There are many ways in which it is possible to do this.

1 If you frequently get colds just before important occasions and often find yourself having to miss dinners or meetings, think carefully. Do you really want to go to those meetings or dinners? Or are you using your colds as an excuse? Is there something about those events which frightens or worries you? If you really wanted to go to those meetings, you would not get so many colds – your body would suppress the symptoms. Only by understanding what it is you are trying to escape will you find out how to avoid getting so many colds.

2 Individuals who lack self-assurance are especially vulnerable to disease and infection. Improve your self-confidence by trying to think of all the good points you have. *See* also pages 94–7.

3 Boredom can increase your chances of getting colds. You need to add purpose and excitement to your life if you are going to minimize your chances of getting a lot of colds. One of the reasons why doctors rarely get colds is that they work with a sense of purpose. Give yourself goals and aims to strive for and your body will become much more efficient at combating germs and infections. If you have a dull, boring job (or no job at all), add purpose and excitement to your life by acquiring a skill or learning a sport that you can dedicate yourself to with enthusiasm.

Convalescence

Wander into any large hospital at visiting time and you'll find it an extremely depressing experience. From the car park to the hospital entrance there will be a phalanx of unhappy-looking men and women, their faces pinched and strained with earnest determination. The men will all be dressed uncomfortably in their Sunday best clothes – squeaky, polished shoes, tight suits and out-of-fashion raincoats. The women will be dressed soberly and respectfully, as though on their way to a funeral.

On the wards the conversations will be subdued and cautious. There will be lots of grave whispering and hardly any laughter. Both visitors and patients will examine their clocks and watches at frequent intervals as though to see just how much longer the whole tedious business of visiting is likely to last.

No one benefits from this sort of encounter – least of all the patients themselves. Abandoned by their visitors, the patients will lie silent and depressed by the encounter. On their lockers will lie souvenirs of these sad visits: bottles of orange squash and doom-laden copies of local newspapers.

The sad irony in all this is that there are now shelves full of evidence showing that if people who are ill or recovering from surgery are made to smile and laugh, they will get better much quicker than they would otherwise. Patients of all ages and all descriptions will, wherever they may be, benefit enormously from hope, encouragement, laughter, merriment, love and affection.

I think that medical professionals have a responsibility to recognize this both in their own approach to medical care, hospital design and internal administration and in their attitudes to visitors. (Hospitals need to be made hospitable – many are far too gloomy and dull.) But whether or not the medical professionals recognize and accept that responsibility, relatives and friends can contribute enormously by developing the right attitude and approach to those who are ill or convalescent.

1   Remember that people who are ill respond very well to humour and happiness. When you visit someone in hospital take with you entertaining presents – books, magazines, comics, puzzles and even toys.

Don't tell them about all the dull and boring and miserable things that have happened to you. Don't take them bills that need to be paid or local newspapers that are full of depressing news about road accidents and deaths. Tell them funny anecdotes about people they know, tell them jokes that you've heard on television and that they might have missed. Entertain them and make them laugh.

2   Remember that all convalescent patients benefit enormously when shown love and affection. Make sure that you keep telling your loved ones that you love them. If you can't visit the hospital, send cards and letters. Send flowers. Telephone and leave a message. Make sure that they know that you care.

3   Be careful not to allow a patient's illness to become a shield, protecting him or her from the future. People often use their illnesses to hide behind. It is often too easy to stay in a sick bed and hide away from the reality of the world. To counteract that potential problem spend some time duscussing future plans. Talk very positively about what will happen when things get back to normal. Start making practical plans for holidays and coming-home parties. Make sure that the patient remembers that there are things to look forward to in the world outside.

Diabetes

Diabetes, or diabetes mellitus to give the disease its full name, is a disorder in which there is too much sugar in the bloodstream. Normally, the food that we eat is broken down by a series of enzymes and acids in our intestines. If the food is rich in carbohydrate, the breakdown products will include sugar and the sugar will end up in our bloodstream. Sugar provides us with energy and we all have a certain amount of it circulating at any one time. Carbohydrates include such varied foodstuffs as bread, potatoes, cake, pastry, biscuits, jam, chocolate, rice, pasta and fruit.

The sugar that we do not need for instant energy is stored in our livers. If too much sugar is already stored there and fresh supplies are continuing to pour in, the excess will be stored as fat deposits. The amount of sugar allowed into the bloodstream at any one time is regulated by a hormone called insulin which is produced by the pancreas gland.

Under normal circumstances, if an ordinary healthy individual eats a packet of biscuits or a box of chocolates and his or her body does not need that much energy, his or her pancreas will pump out a considerable amount of insulin which will ensure that the excess sugar is stored in the liver. If the individual keeps eating biscuits or chocolate and the sugar that is stored is not needed, some of it will be put into long-term storage as fat. In the condition known as diabetes this normally efficient system does not work properly. The production of insulin is inefficient and the amount of sugar circulating in the blood reaches quite high levels.

There are two basic types of diabetes. First, there is the condition in which there is either no or virtually no insulin being produced. This version of the disease normally affects children and is known as child onset diabetes. Second, there is the condition in which there is some insulin being produced, but not enough for the amount of sugar being eaten. In this condition the pancreas still functions but it does not work well enough. This is known as adult onset diabetes. The first of these two types of diabetes usually starts, as its name suggests, in childhood or early adulthood. The second type does not usually start until middle age or later life. The average sufferer from child diabetes will be twelve when he first gets symptoms. The average sufferer from adult onset diabetes will be fifty years of age when he first gets symptoms. Of the two types of diabetes by far the commonest is the adult onset diabetes. Together the two conditions produce one of the commonest of all long-term disorders, with approximately two per cent of the population being affected.

There are a number of different factors which influence any one individual's chances of developing diabetes. Heredity is, without a doubt, the single most important predisposing factor. Your chances of developing diabetes are much higher if you have a family history of the disease. There is also evidence to show that if you are overweight, your chances of developing diabetes are greatly increased. If you are moderately obese, your chances of developing diabetes are increased four-fold. If you are extremely overweight, your chances of developing diabetes are increased thirty-fold. Other factors include race, nationality, age and sex.

Stress, too, can play a very important part in determining whether an individual is likely to develop diabetes. Not only can it increase your chances of developing diabetes, but it can also make it much more difficult for you and your physician to control your disease successfully. When you are under pressure, your body will normally respond by increasing the amount of sugar in your blood, in order to enable your muscles to work more effectively. A good blood sugar level is essential if you are likely to need to respond to any threat or danger. When your blood sugar levels change, the demand for available insulin in your body changes too. The result can be that a stressful situation (or a situation perceived as stressful or potentially stressful) can result in a normally stable case of diabetes becoming unstable and extremely difficult to control.

Once diabetes has developed, it can be controlled in a strictly limited number of ways. In child onset diabetes insulin injections will probably be necessary. In adult onset diabetes tablets may be required to stimulate the pancreas to produce more insulin. In both types of diabetes it is important that the patient controls his intake of carbohydrates and watches his diet and weight carefully. And, again, in both types of diabetes it is tremendously helpful if the individual's exposure and susceptibility to stress can be controlled. It is here that mindpower techniques can be used to greatest effect: helping diabetics and their doctors to obtain and maintain control of threatening and potentially dangerous situations.

1   Restrained emotional outbursts can have a deleterious effect on your body. If you are a diabetic, it is important that you know how to deal safely and comfortably with all extremes of emotional response. *See* also pages 78–82.

2   Learn how to relax efficiently and effectively. Spend a little time learning how to daydream. *See* pages 128–30.

Eczema and Dermatitis

Our skin provides a remarkable reflection of our emotional state. When we are frightened we turn white; when we are embarrassed we go red; when we are anxious our sweat glands work overtime and our skin becomes sweaty and slippery. It is, it seems, always our skin which knows first when there is any confrontation between the body and its environment. It is, therefore, hardly surprising that one of the most important reasons for the high incidence of eczema these days is the increase in the amount of stress in our society.

Eczema, I should explain straight away, is not a single disease. It is, rather, a skin problem caused by a number of different factors, but usually producing a fairly well defined set of symptoms including dryness, redness, itchiness, swelling, blistering and weeping. (Incidentally, there is a good deal of confusion about the difference between the two words 'eczema' and 'dermatitis'. Although some experts claim that there are differences, the two words are more or less interchangeable and can be used to describe much the same type of condition.)

Researchers have found several factors which influence the likelihood of any one individual developing eczema. First, they have found that there is a strong genetic influence. When one parent has eczema as a child, the risk of his or her children developing eczema (or some similar condition such as asthma) is approximately 50 per cent. If both parents have had eczema when they were small, the chances of their child being affected are higher still.

Second, they have found that the personality of an individual can have a powerful influence. They have, for example, found that many eczema sufferers are extremely sensitive individuals who tend to repress their emotions. When upset or sad, they refuse to cry or to let other people see how upset they are. This sort of attitude is apparently commonest among males, who will have almost certainly been taught as boys to suppress their emotions.

It has been found too that eczema sufferers tend to be unusually dependent. As children they will have probably been given a lot of attention when ill, but treated very strictly when fit. It is easy for parents to fall into this trap since it is as natural to be generous and kind to a child with inflamed, sore skin as it is to be keen to balance this with some strictness when the child is feeling a little better. The problem is, of course, that eczematous children may therefore grow up to associate love and affection with poor health and dependence.

Researchers have also found that eczema sufferers tend to be particularly sensitive to stress. We all respond differently to stress and we all have different stress thresholds. It is never the amount of stress we are subjected to that causes the problems so much as our ability to cope with that stress. Eczema sufferers tend to respond badly to relatively small amounts of stress.

Finally, it has been shown that eczema sufferers tend to carry more than their fair share of guilt. They tend to be particularly unselfish and loyal and they worry a lot about what other people think.

Indeed, they worry a good deal about everything: whether or not they are going to have enough money, whether they are doing a good job, whether the people who are close to them are happy. And, of course, they worry about their skin condition.

Not all eczema sufferers exhibit all these personality traits. But the majority of eczema sufferers will probably recognize something about themselves in this list. And if you are an eczema sufferer, you should be able to see which aspect of mindpower to pay most attention to simply by checking out your personality traits.

The aspects of mindpower which are likely to prove most useful for sufferers from eczema, dermatitis and other similar skin problems are listed below. I must stress, as usual, that the eczema sufferer should, in addition to using the mindpower techniques, follow whatever advice is given to him by his medical adviser. There are many useful creams available for the amelioration of eczema – some designed to protect the skin and some to deal with existing or developing skin problems. The mindpower techniques won't necessarily cure an eczematous condition (although they are more likely to cure the condition than any available remedy), but they will minimize the amount of discomfort.

1   Be prepared to let your emotions out, particularly if you are the sort of individual who represses them. Holding in your emotions can lead to all sorts of problems, and your skin will suffer.

2   Learn how to relax your mind properly. Practise when you are not under pressure. *See* also pages 123–31.

3   Build up your confidence. Eczema sufferers tend as a group to have very little self-confidence. *See* also pages 92–7.

4   Ask yourself whether you ever use your eczema to protect yourself from situations which you might find threatening or difficult. If you do, it is important that you investigate other ways of dealing with your problems. If you don't, your eczema will persist.

Headaches

Headaches are so common that four out of every five people reading this book will suffer regularly or occasionally from what is undoubtedly the commonest single medical symptom requiring treatment or advice. They can, of course, be caused by all sorts of different things. You can get a headache if you drink too much alcohol, strain your eyes, have bad teeth, bite ice cream or develop a type of arthritis in the bones of your neck. Some people even get headaches when they have sexual orgasms.

Because headaches can be so excruciatingly painful they can be frightening, and many people who get headaches feel sure that it is a sign of some serious disorder developing, such as a brain tumour. The truth, however, is that brain tumours are exceptionally rare. One expert recently surveyed 1,152 patients referred to a hospital specialist because of headaches. Only one of them had a brain tumour. All had been seen by general practitioners and thought to have possible brain tumours. Obviously, you should always seek expert medical help if you suffer from recurrent, persistent or particularly troublesome headaches. You should also seek medical advice if your headache is accompanied by any other symptoms. Anxiety about a headache can only make it worse and professional reassurance is often as useful a remedy as can possibly be obtained.

The majority of headache sufferers have what are known as tension or stress headaches – these are estimated to account for about 88 per cent of all types of headaches. Tension headaches develop in a very simple way: they are produced by sustained muscle contraction. When certain muscles of the head, neck and scalp are held too tightly for too long, tension headache results. You can see how the problem develops simply by looking around you in a busy office or in a traffic jam. You'll notice that quite a number of individuals will be frowning and squinting with their shoulders hunched and their faces contorted by anxiety. The nervous tension produces muscle tension and that produces the pain.

It may be possible to deal with the pain by taking analgesics such as aspirin or paracetamol. Both drugs will probably prove effective. But mindpower can offer tension headache sufferers a much better long-term solution: a remedy which is often the only permanent, effective remedy.

1   Many regular sufferers have headaches because they are constantly being manipulated into doing things that they really don't want to do.

Norah, a patient of mine in her early forties, was forever complaining of headaches. When I first saw her, she was swallowing a couple of dozen aspirin tablets a day in a desperate and dangerous attempt to control her problem. After talking to her for a while I discovered that Norah's main problem was that she had a very manipulative friend with an extremely powerful personality. Norah's friend had pushed her into serving on a local charity committee, she had pushed her into getting involved with a boys' club, she had pushed her into becoming a member of the Parent–Teachers Association.

Norah wasn't living her own life at all. She was living her life at second hand. It was hardly surprising that all the stress was getting to her and giving her an almost endless series of headaches. When Norah learned to stand up for herself, to explain that she really didn't want to go to a meeting every Monday, every Wednesday and every Sunday and to stand firm under pressure, her headaches miraculously disappeared.

Asserting yourself can be an invaluable way of dealing with nervous tension and with symptoms such as headaches produced by subsequent muscle tension.

2   We often use headaches as an excuse for not doing something that we don't want to do. If we use the headache excuse often enough, eventually our bodies begin to 'give' us headaches on other occasions too. The headache becomes a universal solution to problems that seem to have no answer. Our minds learn to create headaches when confronted with all sorts of problems. The headache becomes a universal answer. If you find yourself using your headache as an excuse, try to identify the real problems which lie behind the excuse.

3   Learning to relax mentally is an excellent way to deal with headaches that have already developed. It is also an excellent way of preventing headaches developing. You can break that chain of events leading from nervous tension to muscle tension by mental relaxation. *See* also pages 123–31.

4   When a headache is caused by muscle tension, then relaxing your muscles will help get rid of your headache. *See* pages 131–3.

Heart disease

Every year in Europe more than a million men and women die of heart trouble. A similar number die in America. In Britain alone more than 60,000 men and women under the age of sixty-five die suddenly and often unexpectedly of heart disease. Men aged between forty-five and fifty-five are most at risk. Although a number of those deaths are caused by heart failure, itself triggered by faulty valves or worn out muscles, most of the younger victims have healthy hearts. They die because the arteries which supply their heart muscles with blood become clogged and unable to carry fresh supplies of food and oxygen.

About the size of a fist, the human heart pumps between 10 and 50 pints of blood every minute, depending on the body's individual needs. To do this the average heart must beat 70 times a minute, 100,000 times a day, 36 million times a year and about 2,500 million times in an average lifetime. The coronary arteries which encircle the heart provide the raw materials which enable the heart to operate and take away the waste products which might otherwise accumulate and cause damage.

There are a number of factors which affect the ability of the cornonary arteries to function efficiently and effectively. Research has shown that people who exercise, such as bus conductors, are less

180

at risk than people who don't such as, bus drivers, and that high blood pressure, excess weight and eating animal fats all increase the likelihood of a heart attack.

Heart attacks can be caused by sudden exposure to cold weather, by a sudden fright or a great surge of excitement. A number of people die every year while watching television programmes. Sporting events such as football matches are particularly likely to cause heart attacks in excited viewers. I remember being called out from home on four separate occasions during one major soccer match.

Smoking damages the coronary arteries since one of the substances in tobacco makes the blood vessels contract. The majority of men who die from heart attacks are cigarette smokers, although there are, of course, exceptions to the rule.

But mental strain is undoubtedly one of the most important causes of heart disease. Three hundred years ago the surgeon John Hunter remarked that his life would be at the mercy of anyone who made him angry. Friedman and Rosenman, the two American doctors who have specialized in the effects of strain on the heart, studied a group of accountants and found that when the April tax deadline approached they were far more likely to have heart attacks.

Researchers who have studied the personalities of heart attack victims have concluded that those who are most at risk are individuals who are ambitious, competitive and hard-working. More important, there is evidence to show that if these individuals learn to relax, their chances of having heart attacks will be reduced.

In a large clinical trial conducted recently 800 men who had had heart attacks were divided into two groups. Those in the first group were given fairly standard medical advice. They were told to cut down on their consumption of animal fats, reduce the number of cigarettes that they smoked and to take the pills which had been prescribed for them. The men in the second group were given more imaginative instructions. As well as being given all the standard advice, they were also taught how to relax, how to deal with emotional problems more safely and how to re-evaluate their aims and ambitions.

Then the researchers sat back and waited to see what happened. Before long a quite startling difference in the health of their two groups emerged. It was found that the men in the second group who had been given advice about relaxation had only half as many second heart attacks as the men in the first group.

I would sincerely and strongly recommend that any patient with a history of heart disease reread Chapter 7. But the following tips are designed to give heart disease sufferers some idea of the ways in which their condition can be helped by mindpower.

1   Men and women who develop heart disease often tend to push

themselves too hard. They work long hours, find it difficult to sit still and relax and often have difficulty in limiting their ambitions. They push themselves into early graves.

If you have heart disease, it is important that you try to establish some proper priorities in your life. How much time are you spending on work? How much time are you spending with your family? And how much time are you giving to yourself? Remember that there isn't a lot of point in earning a million pounds if you are working so hard that you die before you can enjoy the money.

Decide how much money you really need to live happily. Consider how much time you want to spend on your work. Try to allocate time for relaxation and for friendships. Try to put your life into proper perspective.

If you are prepared to make the effort required to understand exactly what you want out of life, you will benefit enormously.

2   Learn how to relax your mind and your body. And be prepared to spend a little time practising relaxation. You can't relax properly simply by flopping down in front of the television set with the day's problems still whirring around in your mind. You wouldn't expect to be able to play golf without practising. So why should you be able to relax properly without practising? *See* pages 123–31.

3   People who develop heart disease are often impatient and aggressive. Do not let your anger kill you. Try to put things into perspective. When you feel justifiably cross, let your anger out. Tell people that you are disappointed with them. A quiet word of protest from you will probably do just as much good as a wild tantrum. And your health will suffer far less. Don't let yourself get over-excited over trivial problems. When the problem isn't worth getting angry about, dismiss it. If you find it difficult to forget, write yourself a memo about it and put the memo into a filing tray. Once a problem has been written down, it is invariably much easier to forget about it. *See* also pages 79–82.

High blood pressure

In order to survive and thrive the tissues and organs of the human body need regular supplies of fresh blood. It is blood that brings the oxygen and other essential foodstuffs without which the tissues would die, and it is blood that carries away the many waste products that are made. To travel around the body, through a complicated network of arteries, veins and capillaries, blood has to be kept under pressure. It is, of course, the heart which maintains that pressure and it does this by regular, rhythmic pumping.

Under normal circumstances several factors affect the pressure at which blood travels round the body. First, there is the heart pump itself. If it is beating unusually rapidly or with exceptional force, that will obviously increase the pressure on the blood. Second, there is the size of the blood vessels and, in particular, the muscular walled arteries. If the bore of an artery has been narrowed by muscular contraction, obviously the blood will have to be put under greater pressure for it to travel through the artery. Third, there is the amount of blood in the body. If the amount of blood increases for some reason, the pressure will rise; if the amount of fluid falls, the pressure will fall.

From day to day your blood pressure changes in response to all sorts of outside influences. So, for example, if you are being physically attacked, your body, recognizing that your tissues need larger amounts of oxygen in order to cope with the crisis, will raise your blood pressure. This temporary variation will help you to stay alive. Once you have escaped, your blood pressure will go back to normal. Such a temporary change in blood pressure is acceptable and useful. It can, quite literally, help save your life.

Unfortunately, blood pressure sometimes goes up and stays up. And that can cause all sorts of problems. The tissues and organs around the body will be subjected to excessive pressures and there is a real risk that they will be damaged. If left unchecked, a persistent rise in blood pressure can kill. It is, for example, a major cause of heart disease and strokes. High blood pressure is one of the major causes of death in the Western world. It has been estimated that up to 20 per cent of the world's population suffers from raised blood pressure.

There are a number of reasons why an individual's blood pressure may be abnormally raised. In some people there may be a genetic influence. In others smoking may be a causative factor. Too much salt or too much animal fat can also cause high blood pressure to develop. But there is little doubt that one of the most important reasons for the current epidemic of high blood pressure is that many millions of individuals are under far more stress than they can reasonably cope with. Stress, it is now clear, causes or exacerbates or influences almost every single case of high blood pressure.

Traditionally, the medical treatment of high blood pressure has involved a number of powerful drugs. Some of these drugs have an important part to play in dealing with and controlling high blood pressure. But today's evidence shows that individuals suffering from high blood pressure can also help themselves by losing excess weight, by avoiding animal fats and cigarettes, by cutting down on their consumption of table salt, by avoiding the consumption of large amounts of coffee and by learning how best to deal with stress and pressure and how best to relax their minds and therefore their bodies.

When used together, these measures will often make it possible for an individual to control his (or her) blood pressure without resort to drugs. And of all these approaches by far the most important is the ability to deal with stress and pressure. It is here that mindpower can help patients suffering from high blood pressure.

By following the advice which follows, many high blood pressure sufferers will, with their doctor's approval, be able to cut down or even leave off altogether, pills which they are taking to control their blood pressure.

1 It is vitally important that all patients with high blood pressure learn how to relax properly, and set aside at least ten minutes every day to do so. *See* pages 123–31.

2 Patients who suffer from high blood pressure are often quite competitive and particularly aggressive. When you feel yourself getting cross ask yourself whether your anger is really justified. If it is, let it out. If not, forget it. There isn't much point in getting excited about an insignificant problem. *See* also pages 79–82.

3 Take a close look at your relationships with others and ask yourself whether any of the problems you have in your dealings with other people could be your fault. Try to analyse your relationships. Ask yourself which of your friends and acquaintances are really important to you. Ask yourself whether you are fair and reasonable with your friends. And ask yourself whether they are fair and reasonable with you. Are you being used? Or are you using other people? By learning as much as you can about your relationships you will learn a good deal about yourself – and about the way that the stresses in your life originate. *See* pages 90–92.

Indigestion

It is your stomach's job to turn the vast variety of assorted foodstuffs that you drop into it into a movable thick soup which can be passed on to the next part of the intestinal tract. The stomach is a vestibule to the rest of the intestinal tract and it is here that food is prepared for digestion. The stomach, it is important to understand, is not just a passive repository for food.

Your stomach helps digest food in two ways. First, the cells of the stomach lining produce something like three litres of gastric juice every day. Of the different substances which make up these juices probably the most important is hydrochloric acid, which is produced by the parietal cells. These exist in the stomach wall in a total population of something approaching a billion.

As a tutor of mine was fond of pointing out when I was a medical student, the acid found in the average stomach is powerful enough to burn holes in your living-room carpet. The effect of these acidic juices is enhanced by the stomach's muscular wall, which churns the food and the juices together before propelling the mixture through a valve into the next part of the intestine, the duodenum. It is these two properties of the stomach which give it its power as a digestive force.

The normal functioning of the stomach depends on a number of different factors: a steady supply of the right sort of food for example. And these days more and more stomachs are malfunctioning. Indigestion is, indeed, so common that if half a dozen people sit down to dinner, the chances are that by the time the coffee is served at least one of them will have indigestion.

A number of different factors can cause indigestion. It can, for example, be caused by eating too quickly. Or by eating the wrong sort of food. If you've ever had to gobble down a meal quickly because you've been late for an appointment, you'll know how easy it is to push more food into your stomach than your stomach can comfortably handle. Or if you've ever tried eating an exceptionally hot Indian meal, you'll know how devastating the wrong sort of food can be.

Too much alcohol or cigarette smoke can cause indigestion too – simply by irritating and damaging the stomach lining and making the whole area more susceptible to damage by the acid that is washing around inside the stomach. But there is a great deal of evidence to suggest that in the majority of cases indigestion is caused by, or at the very least exacerbated by, stress, tension, worry or anxiety.

One of the most dramatic studies of the effect of stress on the stomach was conducted roughly a century ago by Dr Stewart Wolf, who did most of his work with a patient known simply as Tom. As a boy of nine Tom had made the mistake of stuffing some scalding hot clam chowder into his mouth. The hot food had burned his oesophagus so badly that as a result of the incident Tom couldn't swallow food in the normal way; instead an opening had to be made in his abdominal wall so that food could be put directly into his stomach.

When Dr Wolf met Tom he recognized the extraordinary opportunity for research that Tom presented and so he arranged for him to be given a job as a hospital orderly. Dr Wolf then proceeded to study Tom's stomach very carefully indeed. One of the most remarkable discoveries he made was that if Tom was annoyed or angry then the cells in his stomach wall produced huge amounts of quite unnecessary acid. As Tom's face went red with anger so his stomach wall would start to secrete huge amounts of acid.

Excess acid is produced by the stomach lining for an apparently sound physiological reason. The body, recognizing an outside threat of some kind, produces more acid to ensure that any food lying in the stomach is quickly prepared for digestion so that it can be converted into blood sugar supplies as soon as possible. As far as your body is concerned, it is behaving quite rationally. It is responding to an outside threat in the only way it knows how: by preparing it for a fight.

Unfortunately, of course, the excess acid isn't needed and because the threat which has triggered the acid production doesn't go away the stomach continues to produce fairly huge amounts of the acid.

The result is the typical pain and discomfort associated with indigestion, gastritis and other stomach upsets when the acid starts digesting the stomach lining.

The traditional way to deal with indigestion is, of course, to take a tablespoon of white antacid medicine. But that can offer only a very short-term solution. To find a long-term solution you should follow the principles of mindpower. Of course, if your indigestion recurs, persists or remains difficult to control, you should seek medical advice as well as using mindpower.

1   Uncontrolled or badly controlled anger is a common cause of digestive upsets. The indigestion sufferer who fails to learn how to control his emotions effectively may well end up with his indigestion developing into a fully blown peptic ulceration. *See* also pages 78–82.

2   Learn to relax your mind. Don't be tempted to believe that you can learn how to relax in one ten-minute session. To relax properly and efficiently you need to spend some time practising every day. *See* also pages 123–31.

3   Do not let minor irritations annoy you too much. Make a list of priorities in your life. And make sure that you remember what things are important and what are not. *See* also pages 116–22.

4   Do not allow stress or pressure to force you into eating your food too quickly. Make sure that you find time to eat properly and in an unhurried fashion. If you force your food down in unchewed mouthfuls, you are bound to suffer from indigestion. Take a few minutes longer over your lunch and you'll be fitter and stronger for the rest of the day's problems.

5   Try to sort out your relationships with other people. If your relationships often cause you worry and distress spend some time trying to decide just what you can do to solve those problems permanently. *See* also pages 90–92.

6   If you get a bout of indigestion try and imagine that the flow of acid into your stomach is being controlled by a team of special internal 'plumbers' hurriedly turning off the taps through which the acid is pouring. At the same time try to imagine that another team of specialists is busy pouring antacid into your stomach to neutralize

the effects of the acid and prevent further symptoms developing.

Infertility

Infertility is a problem that affects something like one couple in ten. Although it is the female half of the partnership that is usually blamed when children aren't forthcoming, in practice the fault lies just as often with the man.

There are said to be approximately forty possible physical causes of infertility, although you could probably find more if you looked hard enough. Among women, the common problems are a failure of ovulation and a blockage of the fallopian tubes (often caused by some previous infection). Among men, the problems include a failure to produce spermatozoa in sufficient numbers, and a failure to produce spermatozoa of good enough quality. Those disorders can themselves be traced back to other problems in many cases. When a woman fails to ovulate, for instance, the cause may be a specific disorder such as endometriosis or a general complaint such as a considerable or sudden weight loss. When a man doesn't produce enough sperm or produces sperm of inferior quality, the basic cause may be an old infection or even an accident. Mumps is a common enough cause of male sterility. General illnesses such as diabetes and thyroid disorders can also cause infertility; past episodes of venereal disease can be responsible and, occasionally, one partner may develop anti-sperm antibodies.

It is also important to remember that infertility may be a result not of some internal failure but of a simple, straightforward failure to give spermatozoa a decent chance to meet an egg. So, for example, a man who is impotent or who ejaculates prematurely is unlikely to impregnate his partner. Finally, it is worth remembering that frequency of intercourse is also of some significance. The couple who make love once every six months are unlikely to start their family as soon as the couple who make love every day.

Generally speaking, unless a woman is over the age of thirty, it isn't usually necessary to investigate a case of alleged infertility until a couple have been having intercourse without any form of contraception for two years. And well before that time is reached there are several things that a couple can do to enhance their chances of having a child.

Having sex as close as possible to the moment of ovulation is as good a starting point as any. Most women ovulate fourteen days before the end of their menstrual cycle, so sex at that time is far more likely to result in a pregnancy than sex immediately before or after a period. Sex during a period is particularly unlikely to result in conception since not only is there unlikely to be an egg, but also the womb lining isn't in any fit state to receive a fertilized egg. Incidentally, any woman who menstruates regularly is unlikely not to be ovulating. The moment of ovulation can also be timed by keeping a record of the woman's body temperature. A slight fall and rise usually denote ovulation.

To ensure that his sperm are kept in the best possible condition a man should avoid tight jeans, keep out of hot baths and saunas and sit with his legs apart as often as possible. Sperm are very susceptible to heat (that's why the testicles are suspended outside the body).

After intercourse a woman who wants to get pregnant should stay in bed for half an hour, should draw up her knees and should put a pillow under her bottom. These actions are designed to improve the chances of the sperm getting into and through the cervix. The more sperm getting through into the womb, the greater the chance of a pregnancy.

Those are all practical aspects of infertility. But infertility isn't always quite so easy to explain, nor is it always so easy to deal with in a purely practical way. There are, it seems, other hidden factors which have an influence on a woman's ability to conceive.

There is evidence to show that a woman's ability to conceive depends upon her state of mind. In some primitive tribes, for example, it has been claimed that women do not conceive until they have been married and it has become socially acceptable for them to have babies. It seems that this rule applies however many sexual partners a woman has and however long she may continue to have intercourse without using any form of contraceptive.

Startling though this claim may be, evidence from developed countries suggests that it is not as far-fetched as it might at first appear to be. Even in our highly sophisticated society there are many women who claim that they have conceived very quickly after deciding that the time is right for them to start having children. And since hormonal changes in a woman are known to be easily influenced by psychological factors (it is, for example, extremely common for a woman who is worried or nervous to fail to have a menstrual period), it is perfectly possible that conception may be far more readily controlled by mindpower than we had previously imagined.

Since fertility may be governed by mental attitudes, by fears and by anxieties, a woman who is frightened that she will become less attractive to her husband if she gets pregnant may fail to conceive, not because of any physical abnormality, but simply because of her approach and attitude to potential motherhood.

An infertile woman who wants to use her mindpower to help, rather than hinder, her ambition for motherhood should read the following notes, particularly if she is eager to conceive but remains inexplicably infertile.

1 Could you be harbouring any doubts or fears (conscious or unconscious) which might impair your body's willingness to start a pregnancy? Are you worried that your figure will be damaged by having a baby? Are you sure that your relationship will be strengthened rather than weakened by a pregnancy? Are you worried about a pregnancy damaging your career? If you can think of any possible problem which might be produced by your having a baby, you should be aware that your hidden uncertainties may be influencing your ability to become pregnant.

Try to deal with those problems in as straightforward and as honest a way as possible. Talk about the prospects of motherhood with your partner and your employer. Make up your mind positively about your yearnings for motherhood.

2 You may be able to help yourself by thinking about the priorities and purposes in your life. Do you know what things are most important to you? How important is your career? And how important is your family? Difficult though it may be to answer these questions, you must decide exactly where your priorities lie if you are to overcome any hidden barriers to conception.

You may be able to help yourself by deciding that you will work part time for a while and resume full-time employment at some specific future date. Perhaps you should also start thinking now about how many other children you are going to have. (You can always change your mind, of course, but a positive decision now will eradicate any temporary uncertainty.)

3 Think carefully about your relationships. Does your partner want a baby too? Do you have any doubts about your personal relationships? Are there likely to be any new problems with people who will play an important role in your life during and after your pregnancy?

4 Fear can make a woman infertile. Try to eradicate your fears about pregnancy by learning as much as you can about what happens to a woman during pregnancy.

5 Build up your self-confidence. Try to think of the ways in which pregnancy may enhance your appearance rather than damage it (for example, if you think your breasts are too small, pregnancy may enlarge them). *See* also pages 94–7.

6 Learn to relax your mind as thoroughly as you possibly can. There is evidence available to show that women who work under stress may have difficulty in conceiving. *See* also pages 123–31.

Menopausal problems

Between the ages of forty and fifty-five most women reach the menopause. Their glands slow down the production of sex hormones, their ovaries stop producing eggs and their periods cease. They are no longer likely to get pregnant.

The problems that are commonly associated with the menopause are largely caused by the fall in oestrogen levels and the symptoms produced at this time usually include (in order of frequency):

Hot flushes and sweats
Anxiety, depression, irritability, tiredness, sleeplessness
Irregularities of the menstrual period
A fall in sexual interest and some pain on intercourse
Aches and pains – headaches and joint pains being commonest
Hair and skin changes. The skin becomes dry and wrinkles become unusually apparent. The head hair becomes thin and para-doxically hair appears where it isn't wanted – on the face, for example
Inability to remember things and to concentrate
A dry and sometimes sore vagina
A general loss of confidence and a feeling of not being quite so much a woman
Urinary symptoms such as incontinence
A burning or strange taste in the mouth
An increased incidence of broken bones.

Treating the problems which so often accompany the menopause is something of a challenge. Occasionally, of course, if specific problems are troublesome enough, specific solutions can be tried. Calcium supplements will help prevent bone weaknesses. Oestrogen will help give dry vaginal walls more suppleness. And sometimes a mental state of depression accompanying the change will be so severe that anti-depressant therapy will be required.

In addition to the physical problems associated with the hormonal changes produced by the menopause, the average woman in her fifties will be facing changing circumstances which will put her under pressure and will produce stress and anxiety.

These pressures are significant because the hormonal changes which produce the typical symptoms of the menopause – the flushing, the hot sweats and so on – are greatly influenced by the mental attitude of the individual concerned. A woman who is embarrassed by her flushing will go even redder. A woman who fears that her menopausal symptoms are instantly obvious to everyone around will draw attention to herself by her nervous behaviour. A woman who is worried that the cessation of her periods will be accompanied by a vast series of uncomfortable and distressing symptoms will almost certainly suffer from a series of uncomfortable and distressing symptoms. And a woman who is worried about her partner or her children will also suffer more from menopausal problems.

However, just as the symptoms accompanying the menopause can be made worse by each individual's mental approach, so those symptoms can be minimized if the individual has the correct mental approach. The principles of mindpower are designed to enable women to find that right attitude.

1 Many women in their fifties lack purpose. Their children may have left home and retirement may loom ahead. Inevitably, they frequently find their lives without direction. If you are suffering from menopausal problems, ask yourself if your life needs purpose. If the answer is 'yes', try to create new targets, aims and ambitions. Start studying at a local college or take a correspondence course in something that has always interested you. Start up your own business. Take on added voluntary responsibilities.

2 Menopausal symptoms are often made worse by a lack of personal confidence. Work on your self-confidence. *See* also pages 94–7.

3 Use imagery techniques to help overcome your physical symptoms. If you feel that you are getting hot and red, try to think of yourself sitting or standing somewhere extremely cold. Imagine that you are standing in several inches of snow, or plunging into a cold bath or taking part in an Arctic expedition. Your skin temperature will fall and the amount of flushing that takes place will be kept to an absolute minimum.

Menstrual problems

Every month a woman's womb lining builds up ready to receive a fertilized egg. The growth of the lining, or endometrium, is governed by hormones produced by the ovaries. If sperm get into the womb at or around the time of ovulation and an egg is fertilized, the lining will remain where it is. If no egg is fertilized, the cells of the lining will be discharged from the womb ready for a whole new cycle of events to begin. The discharge of the lining makes up the contents of a woman's monthly period.

The length of the average cycle (from the start of one period to the start of the next) is twenty-eight days, but anything between twenty-one days and forty-two days can be regarded as perfectly normal. The important thing is not so much the length of the cycle but its regularity. If a woman regularly has a thirty-five-day cycle, that is normal for her.

191

The period itself, or bleeding phase, usually lasts for between two and seven days. The average bleed lasts for four or five days. Again it is the pattern and regularity that is important. So, if a woman normally has a six-day period, a three-day period will be abnormal for her. And if a woman normally has a three-day period, a six-day period will be abnormal.

Period problems normally fall into one or more of four main categories: absent periods, heavy periods, irregular periods and painful periods. The absence of menstrual periods doesn't always mean that there is something wrong, of course. Young girls who haven't yet reached puberty don't have periods and nor do women who have passed through the menopause. During pregnancy, when a fertilized egg has landed on the endometrium, there won't be any periods. After pregnancy two out of three women who breastfeed their babies still haven't started having their periods again by the time that their baby is three months old.

When there isn't a straightforward explanation for the absence of periods, there can be a number of possible reasons for a woman not to have a monthly bleed. Excessive dieting, anorexia nervosa and some drugs can all stop periods coming when they are expected.

Heavy periods can be caused by a variety of factors. Sometimes the excess blood is produced by hormonal changes. Sometimes an excess bleed can be caused by inflammatory disease, fibroids, an incomplete abortion or an intrauterine contraceptive device. And clearly the first objective must be to identify a specific cause if one can be found. Once the problem has been isolated, a specific medical or surgical remedy may be available.

Irregular periods can be caused by all sorts of problems and always need investigating. They can be caused by hormonal problems, cervical lesions, polyps and a dozen other things. The solution obviously depends upon the cause, but the contraceptive pill is often the answer.

Painful periods are usually divided into two main groups: those which start a year or two after puberty (known as primary dysmenorrhoea) and those which start after years of painless menstruation (known as secondary dysmenorrhoea). The onset of pain in primary dysmenorrhoea usually comes at puberty, and it is caused by the uterine contractions which the production of prostaglandins has inspired. It is a colicky sort of pain, coming a few hours before menstruation, lasting for about a day and sometimes being accompanied by nausea, sweating, fainting and constipation. The pain is usually situated in the lower part of the abdomen and it usually goes into the thighs and lower part of the buttocks. Two thirds of the girls who develop primary dysmenorrhoea have a family history of such pains and many girls who suffer badly have been

192

warned by their mothers to expect a lot of pain and suffering when their periods start. At the very least they will have seen their mothers suffering and learnt to associate periods with pain.

Secondary dysmenorrhoea can be produced in a number of different ways. It always (by definition) develops after years of pain-free menstruation and can be caused by infections, endometriosis, pelvic inflammatory disease, fibroids, polyps, cancer, intrauterine contraceptive devices, bowel disorders, skeletal problems, urinary disorders and just about anything else you can think of.

Of these four types of period problem, the two that are most likely to be alleviated by using mindpower are the first and the last. When periods are missing it is often because the woman concerned is worried about something. Classically the young girl or woman who is worried that she might be pregnant will have a late period or miss one completely.

Under these circumstances there can be little doubt that it is the power of the mind over the body that is having the dramatic effect. And since the period is absent because of the effect of stress on the mind the solution should be clear: the answer is for the woman to relax her mind as effectively as she possibly can. She should spend ten or fifteen minutes three or four times a day deliberately relaxing her mind by daydreaming. She should imagine that she is lying somewhere quiet and peaceful with no worries and no cares. She should feel the warm sun on her face and the soft sand of a warm beach on her back. She should allow the sounds and smells of a sunny day at the seaside to wash away the problems and pressures of her life.

The problems will still be there when she returns from her daydreams, of course. But she will return refreshed and the stress on her body will have been reduced. The result may well be that her periods will resume quite normally.

The other menstrual problem particularly well suited to treatment with mindpower is period pain. Although doctors continue to treat menstrual pains with drugs of many kinds, it has been shown that mental attitudes play a very significant part in the development of this problem. Consequently, analysing and dealing with attitudes, suspicions and anxieties is far more likely to lead to a significant, long-term improvement.

The pains associated with menstruation cause countless thousands of women considerable discomfort every month. The truth is, however, teenage girls are often encouraged to expect their menstrual cycles to be marked by several days of pain. Well-meaning mothers and doctors, and not so well meaning advertisers, all help to perpetuate this suspicion and turn it into an expectation.

Mindpower can help in the following practical ways.

193

1   Imagery is an excellent way to deal with pains of many different kinds. For the specific, abdominal pains associated with menstrual problems there are two techniques which you can try.

First, try clasping your right hand as tightly as you possibly can, imagining in your mind that, as the muscles of your hand contract, so the muscles of your uterus contract too. Try to see your hand as your uterus or womb. Keep your hand like this for a minute or two. Now, slowly relax the muscles of your hand and allow your fingers to unfold. As you do this, your uterine muscles will relax too and your pain will slowly fade away.

Second, as an alternative, imagine that your right hand is as cold as it can possibly be. Try to freeze it so much that it feels quite numb. Then place your frozen hand over the area where your abdominal pain is greatest and let the numbness soak down through your abdominal wall to the site where it is needed most.

2   Learn to relax your mind thoroughly and completely. *See* pages 123–31.

Migraine

Migraine sufferers have to put up with headaches, itchy eyes, stuffed up noses, mood changes, sensitivity to light and noise, and nausea. The headaches, commonly one-sided, can be particularly severe and difficult to treat.

Although there is still some confusion about precisely what happens during a migraine attack, it seems that the problem is largely a result of the body's inappropriate response to stress. Misled into thinking that it can cope with a stressful situation by preparing muscles for direct physical action, the body increases the supply of blood to the muscles and reduces the supply to the brain. Then, when the threat seems to be lifting, the blood vessels to the brain reopen and the blood surges into the tissues. It is this sudden flow of blood which seems to cause the pain associated with a migraine attack.

So far doctors and alternative medical practitioners have all failed to produce any truly useful solutions which can be used to help migraine sufferers. But there are several principles of mindpower which can be applied with good effect.

1   There is a powerful link between stress and migraine – or to be more accurate, what an individual perceives as a stressful problem, and migraine.

Migraine attacks will, therefore, be kept to a minimum by your reducing your exposure to unnecessary stresses. Sort out the real priorities in your life. Make sure that you do not spend too much time dealing with problems and worries which may be of relatively slight importance.

In order to cut down your exposure to unnecessarily stressful situations you may need to assert yourself occasionally. If you constantly find yourself being manipulated into doing things which you find unpleasant or uncomfortable, ask yourself why you succumb to such pressure. Try to understand how others manipulate you and strengthen your resolve to manage your own affairs and create your own order of priorities.

2   Learn to relax your mind. Once you have mastered the technique you will be able to use it whenever you are in a potentially stressful situation. *See* pages 123–31.

3   Migraine sufferers often lack confidence. Consciously build up your self-confidence. *See* pages 94–7.

4   You may be able to get rid of a migraine attack (you will certainly be able to minimize its effects) by using imagery techniques. Since the pain associated with a migraine attack is caused primarily by the constriction of the blood vessels supplying the brain, the aim of any imagery procedure must be to help enlarge the vessels concerned. The trouble is, of course, that it is extremely difficult to open up the arteries supplying the brain – largely because it is difficult to tell just how effective an imagery exercise is, since neither the vessels nor the brain can be seen. However, since the blood vessels to the hands are constricted whenever the blood vessels to the brain are too there is a solution: you must make a conscious effort to direct blood into your hands.

This is easier than it sounds. You simply need to imagine that your hands are getting warmer and warmer. As you do this your blood vessels will open to ensure that more blood goes to the tissues. And as the blood vessels in your hands open, so will the blood vessels to your brain.

Overweight

In half the world the majority of illnesses which kill and disable are caused or made worse by a lack of food. In the other half of the world – the half in which you and I live – the majority of illnesses are caused by or made worse by our eating too much food.

It is impossible to work out precisely how many people die every year because they are overweight – just as it is impossible to work out precisely how many people die because they smoke – but there isn't a shadow of a doubt that obesity is a major cause of death. Overeating and overweight are together probably the single biggest cause of death in the Western world.

If you are overweight, you will be more likely to get high blood pressure, develop heart disease, develop diabetes or have a stroke. In addition, obesity is likely to make your life unpleasant and uncomfortable. It makes crippling diseases such as asthma and arthritis far worse than they need be. And it commonly causes mental problems such as anxiety and depression.

People get fat for a number of different reasons, of course. Some people eat because they are depressed. Others eat because they need comfort. But the one thing all overweight individuals have in common is that they do not listen to their bodies telling them when they have had enough to eat. They do not eat to satisfy their hunger; they eat to satisfy social and emotional rather than physical needs.

Deep within our brains we all have an appetite control centre, itself controlled by the amount of sugar circulating in our blood. This centre can tell us exactly when we need to eat and precisely how much food we need to eat. There is no doubt that if we would only listen to our appetite control centres, we would never get fat. We would eat the right balance of food and the right quantities of food. But we don't listen. We eat for all the wrong reasons.

Think back to when you were small and you'll probably remember that you always ate at fixed meal times. You may well have been encouraged to eat particular types of food. And you were very probably encouraged to finish up all the food on your plate. You were probably told that it was naughty to leave food on the side of your plate when there were people starving in Africa and India who would have been very grateful for the food you didn't really want. Indeed, if you were bottle-fed, your 'training' probably started before you could even sit down at the table and start feeding yourself. Your mother will have encouraged you to keep sucking until the bottle was empty – even if you didn't really want any more. (Breastfed babies are allowed to obey their appetite control centres for the simple but very effective reason that their mothers, while feeding them, can't see how much is left in the container.)

Together all these distorted behavioural patterns help to ensure that you grow up accustomed to overruling your appetite control centre. Eventually your eating habits are controlled not by your body's requirements but by social needs and requirements. You grow up accustomed to the idea of eating at fixed meal times and eating what other people want you to eat. And you eat in the sort of quantities they want to set before you. Look around you next time you eat out – you'll see that most people finish off everything on their plates, however much was put there in the first place. Instead of regulating your appetite by your own needs, you allow your personal eating habits to be controlled by the needs and requirements of others.

You may also have got into the habit of eating while reading, working or watching television. As a result you probably have little idea of what you are eating – or how much – and you just carry on eating until you feel bloated or until everything has gone.

There are several ways in which you can use mindpower to help you regain – and maintain – your natural, healthy weight.

1   Learn to use your intuition to help you tell when you are hungry and when you have had enough to eat. If you listen to your body – and your hunger – and eat only when you need to eat, you will eat in the quantities required by your body.

Get into the habit of eating not according to strict meal times but according to your natural feelings. And, just as important, get into the habit of stopping eating when you are no longer hungry. To do this you must concentrate on what you are doing while you are eating.

2   Learn to be more assertive when you are eating. If you continue to allow other people to determine your dietary intake, you will undoubtedly remain overweight. If you let other people decide how much food to put on your plate, how many portions to give you and when you can stop eating, you will end up with a long-term weight problem. If you are to control your weight permanently, you must learn to control your own intake of food.

Just remember that it is the people who insist on your having a second helping of food who are behaving unreasonably. Imagine what your feeling would be if a friend had the nerve to say 'no' to an overforceful hostess.

3   If you are planning to lose weight, create a sensible weight loss programme for yourself. If you start off with a long-term plan to lose four stone, you will probably lose heart well before you've lost your first stone. The target is too great and too unattainable. Begin with a shorter-term goal – intending to lose say ten pounds – and you will gain your objective far more speedily. The success will give you more confidence and that will boost the chances of your long-term dieting success. You'll think of yourself as a winner.

4   If you want to lose weight from a particular part of your body, try and imagine yourself the shape that you would like to be. Try not to think too much about your large hips, overgenerous bottom or whatever. If you think constantly about your bad points, you will be forcing negative images into your mind and reinforcing your own vision of yourself as an overweight fatty. Try to think instead of the sort of body you would like to have. Think of yourself as slender but shapely. The more realistic you can make this image, the more likely you are to succeed in your weight loss campaign.

197

Pain

The relationship between pain and the mind has been well established for a long time. And it isn't difficult to find practical examples of how a person's mental state can affect the way he feels or responds to pain. You may not approve of boxing as a 'sport', but next time there is a boxing match on television take a look at the two protagonists when the bout comes to an end. Even though both will have received a considerable amount of punishment, and may well be battered and bruised to quite similar extents, the loser will seem to be in much greater pain than the winner.

Or take a look at the athletes who've just completed a race. The winner will look fit and fresh and he'll carry on running round to get the applause of the crowd. The runner who came second will be standing with his hands on his knees, gasping for breath and in obvious pain.

Whatever the source of your pain, there is little doubt that it will be made much worse by worry, anxiety and fear. If you can relax, calm yourself and amuse yourself, it will be reduced. Here are some of the specific ways in which you can use mindpower to help yourself deal with pain.

1   Remember that we all sometimes use pain as an excuse to enable us to avoid unpleasant or difficult tasks. If you suffer from any recurrent or persistent pain that could be associated with some specific responsibility, try to deal with your fears and anxieties about that responsibility, rather than simply attacking the pain.

In other words, if you always get a headache when you have a particular meeting to attend, ask yourself what it is about that meeting that upsets you so much. If you always get a pain in your stomach when certain relatives are due to arrive, you will only obtain a long-term solution to your pain by resolving your conflict with your relatives.

2   Tension and anxiety can make you far more susceptible to pain – and will make any pain that you do feel far more intense. You must learn to relax your mind if you are to lower your susceptibility to pain and increase your chances of defeating pains when they arrive as a result of stress and pressure. *See* also pages 123–31 .

3   Imagery techniques are vitally important in pain control. Relax your mind and then try to imagine that you can see your body's self-healing mechanisms at work. Imagine that you can see the white cells in your blood heading towards the site of your pain and taking with them valuable pain-relieving hormones. Imagine that you can see your white cells patrolling your body as defenders of your peace.

As an alternative try taking yourself outside your body and watching yourself from the other side of the room. Then watch while

198

a nurse soothes your brow and offers you comfort and support. Imagine that there are loving, gentle compassionate people all around you working with you to help ease your pain. When the pain has been banished then return to your body. *See* also pages 133–7.

4   Pain is often made worse by sadness and unhappiness. You can make a small pain worse by mixing with miserable people. Conversely you can reduce the extent of a pain by smiling, laughing and enjoying yourself. Ask yourself whether there is enough fun and laughter in your life. Do you take things too seriously? If your life is too serious, try to find time for more games and for enjoying yourself a little more.

5   Love, care and affection will all help relieve pain. Try to make sure that there is plenty of love and affection in your life. And try to make sure too that no one who is close to you is deprived of love and affection. (You should take care not to offer love *only* when a friend or relative is in pain. If you do then they will gradually come to realize that in order to win your affection they will have to exhibit signs of pain or discomfort.)

Phobias

All of us have our own particular likes and dislikes. One friend of mine doesn't much care for cats. Another has confessed to feeling slightly uneasy when he watches snakes on television. Usually these likes and dislikes are reasonably well controlled but occasionally they can turn into something much stronger – and produce genuine, specific, physical symptoms of anxiety. They become phobias.

People who don't just dislike cats, but who are so scared of them that they become genuinely ill if a cat is around, are said to suffer from ailurophobia. Individuals who can't stand heights are said to suffer from acrophobia. Those who can't cope with horses have equinophobia, and those who get exceptionally and unreasonably frightened of the dark are said to have nyctophobia. Xenophobia is a fear of strangers, pyrophobia is a fear of fire, brantophobia is a fear of thunder, claustrophobia is a fear of confined or enclosed spaces such as small rooms, lifts or cupboards. Agoraphobia – one of the commonest phobias of all – is a fear of going out of doors into open spaces.

When a phobia develops, it is often possible to find some specific reason for it. Someone who is frightened of dogs may well have acquired his fear after some unhappy childhood experience. Someone who has claustrophobia may have acquired that fear after being accidentally or deliberately trapped in a cupboard. A patient with agoraphobia may be frightened to go out of doors because she lacks self-confidence and feels frightened or inadequate when faced with the pressures and tensions of the real world.

Because we now understand how phobias develop, it is quite possible for us to do a great deal to help one another avoid them. When a child is frightened by a dog, it is wise to encourage him to take a mild interest in dogs. If a child falls off a chair, help him back up on to the chair straight away, make a joke about it and keep a tight hold of him so that he will feel both reassured and secure.

When phobias have already developed, mindpower can be used to help find a permanent solution.

1 Phobias often get worse because we allow our imaginations to take over and produce exaggerated fears. It is, however, just as possible to use the imagination to help a patient eradicate a phobia.

A patient with agoraphobia, for example, will be able to lessen her fears by spending some time each day imagining herself walking out of her home, along the street and down the road to her nearest row of shops. She must then imagine herself having a conversation with someone she meets, buying whatever she needs and then returning home. The successful image she creates for herself will enable her to overcome what might otherwise develop into a major social problem.

Similarly, a patient with a phobia of cats should spend some time each day imagining himself first watching cats, then approaching them and finally stroking them. His imagination will have helped create his phobia; it can also help demolish his phobia.

2 People who suffer from phobias suffer from a lack of self-confidence and self-assurance. Any phobic individual should, therefore, spend a little time thinking of a list of all his or her personal virtues. *See* also pages 94–7.

Pregnancy

Pregnancy is not an illness but pregnant women are often treated as though they were ill. And, even more significantly, they are often encouraged to think of themselves as being ill.

Right from the very start of her pregnancy a woman has to visit her doctor, have her blood pressure taken, have a urine sample examined and fill in a form or two. She is given a blood test and told that she'll have to start taking iron tablets. Her friends and relatives will ask her whether she has suffered from any early morning sickness.

Against this background it is hardly surprising that many women do suffer an enormous amount of discomfort and unhappiness while they are pregnant. They are never given a chance to think of the baby they are carrying; they are encouraged only to think of the symptoms from which they are suffering.

Because she is concerned about the risks to her own health the pregnant woman will be under a quite exceptional amount of stress. When the general practitioner looking after her makes non-committal noises after taking her blood pressure, she will leave the surgery terrified that she is going to develop unpleasant complications. When the obstetrician at the hospital mutters something she doesn't understand about her unborn baby, she will spend the next month worrying herself sick (often literally) that there is something wrong.

Under these circumstances it is perhaps surprising not that a few women do suffer from high blood pressure and severe morning sickness, but that so many women manage to get through their pregnancy without any complications at all. In order to get through the months of a pregnancy with the least possible risk of complications developing because of mental pressure, anxiety and worry I suggest that expectant mothers protect themselves in these simple ways.

1   Never be afraid to ask if there is something that you do not understand. Fear of the unknown is one of the most damaging fears of all. If your doctor says something that you don't entirely understand, ask him to explain himself. Or ask someone else to explain what he meant. Do not simply take your fears home with you and allow them to build and grow in your mind. If you do then you will worry yourself into an illness.

2   Always think of yourself as a perfectly healthy woman who happens to be pregnant. Remember that your visits to the surgery and the hospital are probably unnecessary. Unless some abnormality has been discovered (and in the vast majority of pregnancies no abnormality is found), your visits are preventative rather than curative. You are no more ill than you would be when visiting the surgery for a routine vaccination or an insurance medical. If you think of yourself as a patient, you will probably become a patient.

3   Concentrate on the positive, joyful aspects of your pregnancy as much as possible. Remember that many men find pregnant women particularly attractive. Remember that unless you find it painful or uncomfortable, there is no reason why you and your partner should not have sex even though you are pregnant. And remember the baby that you are carrying in your womb. Think of yourself as a mother-to-be rather than someone enduring the agonies of pregnancy.

4   If you develop early morning sickness, remember that it is a common, usually mild condition that rarely requires treatment and does not usually last for long. It is probably caused by nothing more complex or threatening than a simple hormonal change. It can be

helped by avoiding sickly, fatty smells, alleviated with the aid of simple medicines which your doctor can prescribe. It will most likely disappear as your hormone levels change. It is rarely likely to be a threat to you or your baby.

As your pregnancy nears its end you will find yourself facing other problems. There are, indeed, quite a number of culturally conditioned stimuli seemingly designed to ensure that the pregnant woman suffers as much as possible while giving birth. For instance, the natural muscle contractions which she will have when giving birth are not known simply as muscle contractions but as 'labour pains' – a phrase almost guaranteed to ensure that some form of artificial pain relief will be required.

There are a number of ways in which mindpower can be used to lessen the pain and discomfort associated with childbirth.
1   Pregnant women are usually encouraged to spend a good deal of time thinking about the pain they will have to suffer. This medical preoccupation with pain invariably means that pain is a problem during the delivery period. However, by replacing the unpleasant expectations encouraged by doctors with happy thoughts of the baby that is to come, a mother-to-be can often reduce the amount of analgesic that she requires.

I'm not suggesting that childbirth can ever be entirely free of pain, or that there is anything wrong with a woman who feels pain during childbirth. What I am suggesting is that the pain of childbirth can often be helped by replacing negative images with positive ones.
2   Fear produces tension and when muscles are tense they are easily damaged. It is hardly surprising therefore that pregnant women who approach childbirth in a state of fear are more than likely to end up suffering from damaged tissues and requiring medical attention. It always helps if women approaching childbirth learn how to relax their minds thoroughly with daydreaming techniques. *See* pages 128–31.

Sexual problems

Many of the commonest and most destructive sexual problems arise because our early experiences are reinforced and restimulated when circumstances trigger our memories.

A patient of mine called Nicola had tremendous problems with her marriage because she steadfastly refused to let her husband look at her unclothed. When she finally plucked up the courage to tell me about her problem, she actually found it impossible to say the word 'naked'. Not unnaturally her husband found her reticence difficult to understand and even more difficult to accept. He had a fairly normal, healthy sex drive. He didn't expect his wife to take part in any exceptional sexual callisthenics. But he rather fancied the idea of being able to admire her naked body. He got fed up of having to make love to her with the lights off, the bedclothes pulled tight around her chin and her nightdress hardly ruffled.

After talking to Nicola at some length, I discovered that as a girl she had been brought up by extremely strict parents. Her fear of nakedness and her terrible embarrassment had been developed during a series of summer holidays spent by the seaside on the south coast. Unlike other girls of her own age, Nicola had not been allowed to wear a bathing costume (let alone a bikini) but had been made to stay fully clothed on the sand while others were splashing and having fun in the sea. In a rash moment one summer she had hitched up her skirt and paddled her feet in the water, but her father had seen her exhibiting her knees to all and sundry and had sent her back to their boarding house in disgrace.

That incident, and one or two others like it, had established in Nicola a terrible fear of what might happen if she were to allow others to see her body 'unclothed', as she so quaintly and sadly put it. Even as a married woman she couldn't bury those early inhibitions – at least not until after a great deal of discussion and baring of her soul.

Nicola's problem was rather exceptional, but it was by no means unique. And although few of us are quite so inhibited, most of us have inhibitions of our own. We feel embarrassed at being touched or seen naked by strangers or by members of our own sex. Our responses come, as do so many feelings, from what we have learnt as children.

When we are young, we sense when adults are excited, stimulated, shocked or disgusted by things that they have seen and we learn to respond accordingly. Our sexual anxieties, fears and tensions are all created by those whose actions we followed and respected when we were young. It is perhaps hardly surprising that in later life pleasure and fear so often come together when sexual feelings are aroused.

In order to deal successfully with your own sexual problems, you must first try to discover what forces have been involved in helping to form your own tastes, predilictions, ambitions and weaknesses. Try to identify your personal attitudes towards sex and then search through your past memories looking for possible links and explanations. Your sexual tastes will have been moulded by your parents, your teachers, your friends and your earliest sexual partners.

What you learnt as a child will influence your attitudes and preferences as an adult. So, for example, if you were discovered in the act of making love on the living-room carpet, you may, in later years, find that a most stimulating memory. You may find yourself powerfully stimulated by the thought of making love on the living-room carpet. On the other hand, of course, you may remember the incident with such shame and horror that the very thought of it still makes you quite impotent with fear. If your parents disapproved of sex and taught you that it was something rather dirty, you may only be able to obtain real sexual gratification by having secret assignations in seedy surroundings.

Whatever sexual problems you may develop (and whatever the reasons for those problems), you will very probably be able to use mindpower to help you in a number of ways. These techniques can be used either in conjunction with professional advice or by themselves.

1   You may be able to improve your sexual potency or appeal by learning to fantasize. There is a powerful link between sexual appeal and physical danger and you may be able to use these links to enhance your personal sexuality.

If, for example, you imagine that you are involved in a fast car chase and that your life is repeatedly endangered, your body will respond to the imagined danger. Your heart will beat faster, your pupils will enlarge, your face will become flushed and you will sweat a little. All these changes are also signals which suggest a high level of sexual arousal and you will, therefore, appear more attractive to members of the opposite sex.

2   If you are male and you have difficulty in having an erection, fantasizing will probably help you. Think of a woman whom you find distinctly attractive and then imagine her making overtures towards you in circumstances which you find appealing. Allow your mind to roam free and unfettered. Imagine that she undresses herself and then you. Allow your imagination to construct a powerfully erotic screenplay.

3   The other common male problem (apart from impotence) is premature ejaculation. You should be able to conquer this problem by creating a non-erotic fantasy in your imagination. As you start making love, imagine that you are doing something distinctly non-arousing – checking your accounts, for example. Or doing some gardening. Your imagination's dull fantasy will slow down your sexual response.

4   Many sexual problems are caused by a lack of self-confidence. Make a list of your sexual strengths, physical virtues and personal achievements. Think of the aspects of your personality which are sexually appealing. Imagine ways in which others might find you particularly attractive. Invent a role for yourself as a sex symbol. *See* also pages 94–7.

5   If you have difficulty in initiating or maintaining sexual relationships, ask yourself what goes wrong with your relationships with

other people. Do you expect too much? Do you promise too much? Do you promise too little? By asking yourself such specific questions about your sexual relationships, you should be able to find where the faults lie.

Sleeplessness

Every night millions of people take pills to help them get to sleep. But, sadly, many of those sleeping pills cause more problems than they solve. If you take sleeping tablets for more than a week or two, you are quite likely to find yourself needing to increase your nightly dose of drugs for the simple reason that sleeping tablets can actually produce insomnia when taken for more than seven days or so.

If you have difficulty in sleeping at night, your first task should be to find out exactly why you have difficulty in sleeping. Once you have identified the cause of your problem, there may well be a very simple solution.

Answer these simple questions.

1 Are you currently taking a sleeping tablet or tranquillizer?
If you are then the pills you are taking may well be contributing to your problem. Talk to your doctor about reducing the dose of your tablets, but remember that sleeping pills and tranquillizers need to be reduced under medical supervision. To 'kick' your habit you will need to reduce your nightly dose of pills as gently and as cautiously as you can. You should aim at halving your dosage every fortnight.

2 Are you kept awake by pain?
If you are, you must attempt to treat the cause of your pain. Discuss your problem with your doctor. If he is unable to help you and you cannot get rid of your pains yourself, ask for a second opinion.

3 Are you kept awake by any other symptoms such as breathlessness or cramp?
If you are, you need to visit your doctor for help and advice.

4 Do you have difficulty in getting to sleep because you are too hot or too cold or because you are in some other way uncomfortable? If you have answered 'yes' to any of these queries, you must make whatever adjustments are necessary to your sleeping arrangements.

5 Are you kept awake by noise?
If so, try soundproofing your bedroom with bookshelves and double glazing. Or try wearing ear plugs.

6 Are you currently trying to lose weight?
People who are slimming seem to get less sleep than others. Their low blood sugar seems to keep them awake.

7 Do you get kept awake by hunger?
If so, have a bite of supper. Don't have anything hot, rich or spicy. A

glass of milk and a biscuit should do fine.

8 Do you have to get up at night to pass urine?
If you do, avoid alcohol, tea, coffee and other drinks during the evening. Empty your bladder before retiring. If the problem persists, see your doctor.

9 Do you usually take a nap in the afternoon?
Your inability to get to sleep at night may simply be the result of the fact that you are sleeping too much! Cut out the afternoon nap.

10 Are you depressed?
When depression and sleeplessness go together it is the depression that needs a doctor's treatment.

11 Do you worry because you don't sleep as much as other people you know?
Some people need nine hours sleep a night. Others only need five hours. There is no perfect figure.

12 Do you worry because you don't sleep as much as you used to?
We all need less sleep as we grow older.

13 Do you take any prescribed drugs at all?
Then have a word with your doctor. Some drugs may produce sleeplessness.

If you have still not found a specific reason for your insomnia, it may well be that you are going to bed at night with the day's worries and anxieties buzzing around in your head. If that is the case, it is hardly surprising that you are having difficulty in sleeping. The day's stresses need to be eradicated. Even if you get to sleep with so many problems on your mind, you will probably sleep fitfully since your mind will spend the nocturnal hours playing with all the problems you have left lying around.

In order to rest and relax your mind thoroughly so that you will sleep properly follow this simple mindpower programme.

1 Relax your body thoroughly before getting into bed. Begin by taking a good brisk walk for ten or fifteen minutes and try to walk as fast as you can. Try to think through any of your day's problems. When you get back from your walk, take out a notebook and a pencil and write down all your problems and worries. Keep that notebook by your side from now on. Every time a new problem or thought pops into your head write it down.

2 Have a soothing, warm bath for another ten or fifteen minutes. Allow your mind to float quite freely as you bathe. If any fresh thoughts or ideas pop into your head, write them down in your notebook.

3 Go to bed with a relaxing book. This is designed to eradicate the day's troubles from your head. Make sure that you take any pain-killing tablets that have been prescribed for you. Read your book for ten or fifteen minutes. (Making love is an excellent but optional

alternative.)

4 Before you lie down, turn off the lights. It helps, incidentally, if your bed is warm. If you have used an electric blanket, make sure that it is turned off.

5 As soon as you lie down close your eyes and create for yourself a soothing relaxing dream. *See* pages 128–31.

Smoking

It all started when Christopher Columbus received a gift of tobacco leaves from the natives of San Salvador and brought them back to Europe. Gradually through the centuries which followed, chewing and smoking tobacco spread in popularity all around the world. The habit really caught on, however, when machine-rolled cigarettes were introduced less than a century ago. The introduction of neatly rolled cigarettes led to women starting smoking too.

During the many years that it has taken to reach its present popularity tobacco has been investigated by scientists on many, many occasions. In 1928 researchers isolated nicotine and identified it as an active ingredient of tobacco that was particularly poisonous. Surprisingly there is enough nicotine in an average cigar to kill two people. The only reason why cigars and cigarettes aren't instantly lethal is that the nicotine they contain is taken into the body fairly slowly over a period of time.

In addition to its poisonous qualities, nicotine has a number of effects on the human body. It stimulates the central nervous system and increases electrical activity in the brain, it lowers the skin temperature, causes blood vessels in the skin to narrow, increases the blood pressure and the heart rate and numbs the taste buds on the tongue.

Since it has so many effects on the human body it is perhaps hardly surprising that tobacco is now known to cause or make worse a considerable range of disorders. We tend to think of it as being only the cause of lung cancer, bronchitis and other types of chest infections. But, in fact, smoking is a powerful and important cause of heart disease and high blood pressure. Smoking narrows the arteries and decreases the efficiency of the human heart. A high proportion of the younger men who die from heart disease smoke.

Smoking is also a major cause of stomach ulcers, gastritis and indigestion. Cigarettes have an irritating, damaging effect on the stomach, they help to produce ulcers where there are none and they help to prevent the healing of ulcers that are already present.

Many smokers dismiss the dangers of smoking by arguing that they have known heavy smokers who have been unaffected by tobacco. One man I once met, for example, insisted that his father had smoked fifty cigarettes a day for half a century without having any physical illness at all. That is rather like arguing that because some people have survived serious car crashes without injury, there is no danger in being involved in a serious car crash.

Those who claim that smoking is a harmless activity are, of course, encouraged by those representatives of the tobacco industry who are, for their own quite obvious reasons, anxious to deny the evidence that exists. Few commercial lobbying groups are quite as powerful as the tobacco industry. And few governments are able to be entirely ruthless when it comes to dealing with the tobacco industry. In Britain, for example, the tobacco industry contributes something like £4,000 million every year in taxes. It is difficult for any government to ignore the claims and protestations of such an important tax payer.

But despite all the discussion about whether or not tobacco is dangerous, a growing number of people are now struggling to break the powerful hold that tobacco can have. Convinced by the evidence they have seen and read, and convinced too no doubt by the fact that they have noticed their own health being damaged by tobacco, hundreds of thousands of smokers are struggling to give up tobacco each year. It isn't easy, of course. Smoking is just as addictive as drinking alcohol or using heroin.

Many give up smoking for a short period but within a matter of weeks or months they are smoking again. They fail not because they are lured back by an unbroken physical addiction, but because they have never come face to face with the reasons which led them to smoke in the first place.

If you are planning to give up smoking, you must first find out precisely why you do most of your smoking. Occasionally, it is perfectly true, you will smoke to be sociable, or because someone has offered you a cigarette and you have accepted one without really thinking about it. But most of the time when you smoke, you do so to help yourself deal with quite specific problems of one sort or another. You may smoke when you are under a tremendous amount of pressure, for example. Or you may smoke when you are bored.

If you don't find out exactly what those problems are and why you smoke, and you don't find other ways of dealing with those problems, then your chances of giving up tobacco permanently are very limited indeed. Mindpower, however, can help you a great deal.
1   If you tend to do most of your smoking when you are under stress or pressure, try to think back to one particular occasion when you can remember smoking and remember being under a tremendous amount of pressure. Try to see the room that you were in and the people you were with. Try to smell the furniture polish and the stale

208

cigarette smoke. Now try to recreate the fears, the anxieties and the apprehensions which were with you as you sat in that room. Try to feel the dryness in your mouth and the sweat on your hands. Try to remember what it was that you were so worried about.

When you have succeeded in creating the background for yourself, try to step back and see yourself sitting in that room. Become an invisible stranger standing in a far corner of the room just watching yourself. And now watch yourself coping perfectly well without needing to light up a cigarette. Watch yourself dealing with all the problems which come up. And watch yourself coping perfectly adequately without the need for a cigarette.

If you practise this imagery technique regularly, you will gradually replace your accustomed image of yourself smoking when under pressure with an image of yourself coping perfectly well without a cigarette.

2 If you do a great deal of your smoking when you are bored, there are two techniques which you can try. First, simply try imagining yourself sitting quiet and still and coping very well with boredom without smoking. See yourself sitting at the breakfast table calmly reading your paper but without a cigarette between your fingers. See yourself sitting on a train without a cigarette in your hand. Create this image of yourself as often as you possibly can and you will gradually build a picture of yourself surviving boredom without tobacco.

Alternatively, try filling your mind with exciting fantasies the next time you are feeling bored. You will, in this way, conquer your boredom and banish your need for a cigarette. Try to see yourself making love to someone you find extremely attactive. Imagine yourself doing something daring, exciting and glamorous.

3 If you decide that you do most of your smoking because you lack self-confidence, read pages 94–7. As you build up your confidence, your need for cigarettes will gradually disappear.

(Note You can use the above techniques to help you conquer other bad habits such as nail biting and stuttering.)

Index

211

214